Preconscious Foundations
of Human Experience

PRECONSCIOUS FOUNDATIONS OF HUMAN EXPERIENCE

TRIGANT BURROW

Edited by William E. Galt

Foreword by Nathan W. Ackerman

Basic Books, Inc.
Publishers
NEW YORK   LONDON

FOREWORD

It was in the garden of a madhouse that I met a youth
with a face, pale and lovely, and full of wonder.
   And I sat beside him on the bench, and I said
"Why are you here?"
   And he looked at me in astonishment and he said, "It is
an unseemly question, yet I will answer you." . . .
"Each (father, mother, teacher) would have me but a
reflection of his own face in the mirror."
"Therefore I came to this place. I found it more sane
here. At least I can be myself."
   Then all of a sudden he turned to me and he said,
"But, tell me, were you also driven to this place by
education and good counsel?" And I answered, "No, I am
a visitor."
   Then he said, "Oh, you are one of those who live in the
madhouse on the other side of the wall!"*

D AY BY DAY in the present crisis, it is dinned into our
heads that a world divided cannot stand, but that is how it is—
a world wracked by conflict, flooded with madness, menaced
by mass destruction. Senselessly, we keep battering away at
human differences as if to abolish them. Rather we should
prize them. The challenge is clear. If we would survive, there
can be but one answer; we must find a way to come together
to create one world, a family of man. But how?

* Kahlil Gibran, "The Mad Man," *The Wanderer* (New York: Alfred
A. Knopf, 1932), pp. 42 f.

A storm is brewing. We are frightened, all of us. Yet, we drift, helpless, hardly daring to move. Under this dark cloud, it is fitting that we should call to mind the name of Trigant Burrow. Here was a man who, a generation back, divined the danger, not as a war of political systems, but rather as a vast sickness of human relations, a mental aberration, global in scope and encompassing all humanity. Burrow struggled his entire life to understand that worst of all plagues—man against man.

In accepting the invitation of The Lifwynn Foundation to write the Foreword to this posthumous work of Burrow, I feel that I am given a deep trust. As far back as the 1920's and 1930's, Burrow made some startling discoveries. "He was called upon to shatter many cherished prepossessions regarding human behavior and to make some of the most unwelcome statements of our time."* The reaction to Burrow and his studies in mental health is a strange and mysterious tale. His writings were provocative, piercing, even shocking; they were shelved. Presently, some thirty years later, the same ideas, one by one, are being rediscovered. They represent now, in essence, the vanguard of a new social-psychiatric approach to mental health, the core of an advancing science of human behavior. Why, for the major part of a half century, were Burrow's theories by-passed?

Who is this man, and by what odd fate were his early discoveries buried? Only a few years back, I had not so much as heard his name. Could this have been simply my personal ignorance? Stirred to curiosity, I made inquiry among my colleagues in psychiatry. They were mainly as uninformed as I. It is true, some had a vague recollection of his writings, but they seemed to dismiss him quickly as one who had gone off the path. This seemed very odd. How could this giant figure have remained so obscure, and for so many years?

---

* *A Search for Man's Sanity*, "The Selected Letters of Trigant Burrow" (New York: Oxford University Press, 1958), Preface by the Editors, p. xvi.

How I came to learn of Burrow and his works is another story. In 1953, I reviewed a book called *Our Common Neurosis,* by Charles B. Thompson and Alfreda P. Sill, students and co-workers of Burrow. In 1957, I had occasion to write a comment for the Oxford University Press on a selection of Burrow's letters, later published under the title, *A Search for Man's Sanity.* After that, through the good graces of The Lifwynn Foundation and Burrow's dedicated co-workers, Drs. Hans Syz and Charles B. Thompson and Mrs. William Galt, I was given free access to Burrow's abundant writings. Finally came the invitation to write the Foreword to this volume. For me, this study of Burrow's life, his work, his writings was a deep and rewarding personal enlightenment.

In reading *A Search for Man's Sanity,* I had a feeling akin to *déjà vu,* a sense of recognition and awakening of a kind experienced perhaps once in a lifetime. Burrow's imaginative concepts evoked in me a powerful confirming echo. With a dignity, integrity, and honesty that are rare, Burrow indicted the abnormality inherent in so-called normal behavior, the greed, the hoarding, the murderous competitiveness. From my own clinical work, I knew all too well the features of "the social neurosis." Burrow's mind seemed like a mirror of a whole generation of thinkers grappling for an answer to the irrational destructiveness of man's relation to man.

But how was I to understand this piece of history: Burrow dismissed from his university appointment, excommunicated from the American Psychoanalytic Association, and then a virtual taboo placed on his name? Burrow, a dedicated researcher in human behavior, tossed into scientific exile! Was this some peculiar quirk, an odd accident of history? This could hardly be. I could explain it in only one way.

A generation ago, Burrow's theories were far in advance of his time. They were too radical, too threatening to conventional systems of thought. By Burrow's own admission, even he felt inwardly threatened by his discoveries concerning the pathology of normality—his ideas must have been felt to be a danger to the then-popular concepts of psychiatry and psycho-analysis. Even more important, his approach challenged the established self-identity of investigator and therapist, and the implications of his theories for a revolution in established social forms were possibly such as to impel what amounted to a mass avoidance, an unconscious complicity in protest and denial. This is surely one of the strangest episodes in the history of psychiatry.

But the truth will out. Now comes a curious and paradoxical shift. One by one, Burrow's concepts begin to re-emerge in the current literature, but oddly enough, not as coming from him. Piecemeal, they reappear and gain strength in the writings of contemporary scholars in the field of mental health.

Burrow died in 1950. Beginning in 1909, he trained with Adolf Meyer and Carl G. Jung, and for some years he faithfully followed the teachings of Freud. Then, in the early 1920's, he took a different tack. He evolved a method of group analysis and spent his life exploring the manifestations of "the social neurosis." At heart, he was neither rebel nor slave. He had no urge to rebel for the sake of rebelling, no yen to pit one system of thought against another, but rather to bring about a convergence of the elements of truth. But neither was he slave to popular fashions and theories. After years of testing Freudian doctrine, he was convinced that something was wrong, something missing. He devoted himself to what he might discover of the neurosis, not of the isolated, single mind, but rather of the human species as a whole. He became concerned with the madness of humanity.

Burrow's main theoretical contributions may be sketched as follows:

(1) The neurosis of society is primary; the neurosis of the individual, secondary.

(2) Normality must be distinguished from health. Normal behavior is a brand of shared sickness. The characters of the so-called normal person and of the neurotic are not essentially different.

(3) Fundamental to human nature is the principle of the biosocial union of mother and infant, of individual and group. The phenomenon of primary preverbal identification is the core of Burrow's theory of the preconscious foundation of human experience. "The preconscious mode" is a basic oneness and unity, it is the "I and thou," the "thee and me." Basic to all else in the development of mind is a current of physiological continuity of child and mother, person and world.

The failure to maintain a healthy preconscious union in the early phase of development results in a process of deformed weaning, a kind of sick individuation which fortifies the divisive, separative, oppositional trends. It produces the split personality. It foredooms the individual to aloneness. It cripples vitality and the creative unfolding of the person in society.

(4) Cooperation and joining in human relations rest on a more fundamental principle than do competitiveness, separateness, and destructive exploitation.

(5) The progressive misuse of image and language in human development is linked with the distortion of biosocial union. Intellect and word are split from emotion and body. The "I"-persona emerges as a false expression of individuality.

(6) The trend toward mental illness is paralleled by a shift to the physiological pattern of ditention, a deviant internal attitude which can be discriminated from the primary pattern of cotention. The quality of subjectivity—the mood and perceptual experience—is distinct in the two physiological modes and can be utilized to reactivate the healthy pattern of cotention.

Now let Burrow speak for himself:

Man is not an individual, his mind is not individualistic, he is part of . . . the primary or racial continuum.*

* "The Laboratory Method in Psychoanalysis, Its Inception and Development," *The American Journal of Psychiatry*, V (1926), 348 f., as quoted in the Editor's Preface, *Preconscious Foundations of Human Experience*, p. xix.

The preconscious mood . . . is a common experience that finds expression in all the various phases of man's activities— in the distorted dreams and symbols of the neurotic and psychotic as well as in the creative productions of the poet, artist and scholar.*

Individual discord is but a symptom of social discord. The reactions of the neurotic are the direct issue of our so-called normal society.

. . . The widespread perversion of the human spirit . . . has caused the hideous distortion of values embodied in the repressive subterfuge and untruth of our so-called moral codes and conventions.†

Of course, "I"-personae do get together socially. They pool their affects and prejudices in the formation of families, working groups, communities, political parties, nations, etc. But no matter how large the social extension, the amalgamation is not a true integration. . . . The inflexible core of "rightness" and all-might determines the behavior of the individual. It results in the assumption of a type of difference and hostility for which there are no biologically valid grounds.‡

Burrow's entire life work was dedicated to a quest for the causes of mental illness. The direction of this search, however, moved from outside inward, from society and culture back to the individual mind, rather than the other way. He was a prime founder of the culture–personality school of thought. In his original distinction between normality and health, he opened a vast area of investigation of the relation between human values and mental health.

Today, the extent of corroboration for Burrow's concepts is remarkable. One may mention in passing the work of Karl S. Lashley, Kurt Goldstein, Kurt Koffka, Ludwig von Bertalanffy, Peter Kropotkin, George H. Mead, Ruth Benedict, Kurt Lewin,

---

* From Burrow's original draft for *Preconscious Foundations of Human Experience* as quoted in the Editor's Preface, p. xix.

† *Preconscious Foundations of Human Experience*, p. 351.

‡ *Science and Man's Behavior* (New York: Philosophical Library, 1953), p. 64.

Lawrence K. Frank, Harry Stack Sullivan, Erich Fromm, Gardner and Lois Murphy, and many others.

From his associates of The Lifwynn Foundation, which is still active, and particularly from his professional co-workers, Hans Syz and the late William E. Galt, Burrow gained precious and skillful support. Galt provided especially vivid and convincing documentation of the primacy of cooperation in human behavior. "We have found much evidence that cooperation is a fundamental property of protoplasm itself."*

A rousing affirmation of Burrow's theory is to be found in Walter B. Cannon's *The Wisdom of the Body.*

> The welfare of the large community and the welfare of its individual members are reciprocal. . . . The homeostasis of the individual human being is largely dependent upon social homeostasis. . . . [T]he social organism, like the bodily organism, cannot be vigorous and efficient unless its elements are assured the essential minimal conditions for healthful life and activity.
>
> Is it not possible that social organization, like that of the lower animals, is still in the rudimentary stage of development? It would appear that civilized society has some of the requirements for achieving homeostasis, but that it lacks others and, because lacking them, it suffers from serious and unavoidable afflictions.
>
> [T]he [individual] organism suggests there are early signs of disturbance of homeostasis. . . . These warning signals are little known in the social organism, and yet their discovery and the demonstration of their real value would make contributions to social science of first-rate importance.†

I am convinced that Burrow made precisely this contribution. Steadily, the evidence mounts in biology, ethology, social psychology, anthropology, and psychiatry to substantiate Burrow's main thesis of a primary biosocial union, a funda-

---

* William E. Galt, "The Principle of Cooperation in Behavior," *The Quarterly Review of Biology,* 15 (1940), 401–410.

† (New York: W. W. Norton & Co., 1932), pp. 292, 295, 304.

mental principle of cooperation in human relations. Burrow was correct in alleging that, in the evolution of society, this principle has somewhere been pathogenically aborted and derailed.

Regarding the classical Freudian theory, I am convinced of a strange paradox. Despite the exquisite brilliance of Freud's foray into the whole field of human sexual behavior, he somehow by-passed a significant problem. It seems to me he got derailed in his evaluation of some aspects of the sexual drive. Just as all is not gold that glitters, so, too, everything that looks like sex is not sex. I believe that Freud failed to read correctly those kinds of human behavior in which sex is a disguise of other motives. In such instances, sexual action turns out to be merely the instrumentality for the discharge of aggression and competitive power-striving.

I cannot agree with Freud's definition of perversion. It is my view that any form of sexual act, including the heterosexual one, can under special circumstances represent a perversion. My criterion for perversion is a simple one. It is the perversion of a relationship from its primary purpose of love to purposes of mastery, enslavement, or destruction of the partner. I believe that human relations are degraded when a dichotomy between sex and tender sentiment sets in. The capacity for love is not a late development in the Oedipal phase of personality, as Freud believed; rather, it exists *de novo* in the newborn infant. The tender response is there to begin with; it becomes crushed and twisted secondarily, as a consequence of sick family relationships.

Several other pointed observations made by Burrow hold a special historical interest. In studies of human behavior, it is essential to take fully into account the observer's own bias, the elements of sickness in his personality; beyond that, one must consider the influence of the observer's participation in the very processes of sickness he undertakes to study. In essence, the subjectivity, the relativity, the emotional distortions of the professional observer need to be considered as well as the warped behavior of the sick patient. It was this conviction that impelled Burrow, as far back as 1918, to enter into a mutual analysis with his student-assistant—later his lifelong co-worker —Clarence Shields. This was the birth of the method called group analysis.

Noteworthy in this connection is one odd, but persistent, fashion in the development of psychotherapy. Characteristically, the therapist offers a comprehensive report of the patient's behavior, but does not include his own. He omits an explicit, systematic consideration of his participant role. He excludes himself in the examination of the therapeutic process. He is in hiding. These are strong words, but true. This tradition, deeply rooted, has hampered the evolution of a comprehensive theory of therapeutic technique.

But now it is changing. The dynamic of therapeutic process is being reconceptualized as a circular interchange of emotional influence. The role of the therapist, "countertransference," and the significance of a particular pairing of patient and therapist are given greater recognition.

Consider, for example, the relevance of the following quotation from the published paper of an internationally known analyst:

> The further we penetrate in our analyses, the more we find that we are dealing with problems which involve everybody. . . . This disturbing thought occurred to me long ago: does the analyst defend himself by his very profession as a psychoanalyst, by analyzing others? I kept it carefully to myself. . . . I felt no wish to publish on this subject.

He then alludes to Freud's idea that

> one may be justified in considering whole epochs of civilization, perhaps whole humanity as neurotic (as Burrow had maintained). . . . Freud states that ". . . one day somebody

will dare to undertake the pathology of cultural communities." . . . The original neurotic manifestation in the childhood situation is but a symptom of a total constellation, a family neurosis so to speak.

Modern biology itself moves in the direction of a better recognition of cultural or social inheritance. . . . Modern research shows that much of what appeared to be biological inheritance is in fact cultural inheritance transmitted socially.*

Challenging, indeed, is the comment on Burrow's theories by D. H. Lawrence. In 1927, in a published review of *The Social Basis of Consciousness,* he wrote:

Dr. Burrow is that rare thing among psychiatrists, a humanly honest man. Not that practitioners are usually dishonest. They are intellectually honest, professionally honest, all that. But that other simple thing, human honesty, does not enter in, because it is primarily subjective; and subjective honesty, which means that a man is honest about his own inward experience, is perhaps the rarest thing, especially among professionals. . . .
Dr. Burrow has struggled through years of mortified experience to come to some conclusion nearer the mark. And his finding is surely much deeper and more vital and, also, much less spectacular than Freud's.
Mankind at large made a picture of itself, and every man had to conform to the picture, the ideal. . . . This is the great image or idol which dominates our civilization, and which we worship with mad blindness. The idolatry of self. . . . And according to the picture, each one is a little absolute unto himself, there is none better than he. Each lives for his own self-interest. . . . [T]oday, all is image consciousness. Sex does not exist, there is only sexuality. And sexuality is merely a greedy, blind self-seeking."†

* S. H. Foulkes, "Psychotherapy 1961," *British Journal of Medical Psychology*, 34 (1961), 91–102.

† "A New Theory of the Neuroses," *The Bookman*, LXVI (1927), 314–317; republished in *Phoenix*, "The Posthumous Papers of D. H. Lawrence" (New York: The Viking Press, 1936).

Basic to the test of the validity and value of Burrow's ideas are two fundamental questions. How do we view the individual man? How do we view the aggregate of human beings in society? Is it true that only individuals in isolation express the functions of mind? Or can we validly search for an operational definition of something like a group mind? Surely, we must draw clear distinctions between the operations of the individual psyche and the behavior patterns of a social group. The psychological principles that govern the individual mind and those that govern the behavior of the group differ. And yet, without the group, without social interaction, there can be no mind as we know it.

Long ago, Spencer advanced the idea that human society is an organism made up of individuals, just as the body of the individual is made up of cells. At that time, Spencer's theory, lacking support from biology, was dubbed "the group fallacy." And, since that time, it has been the fashion to insist that groups do not behave, families do not behave; only individuals think and feel. But the same problem, essentially unsolved, hangs on doggedly. Man is a social animal; mind is a social and contagious function.

What, after all, is the individual? Is mind the separate expression of the individual? Or is mind fundamentally the organization of interpersonal experience, the product of a person's growth as part of a family, community, and humanity as a whole? The issue cannot be the individual versus the group. The individual man either grows out of the social man or he just does not grow.

And who is sick—the individual, the family, society? What do we mean when we exclaim with horror that our world is going mad?

We must rethink this whole question. Evidence accumulates in the field of biology and the science of human relations to support the importance of a basic current of social interdependence and cooperation throughout animal forms. Burrow's theory rests on firm biological ground.

As Galt writes in "The Principle of Cooperation in Behavior":

> Contrary to our beliefs, our fancies and our cherished suppositions, the individual does not constitute the unit of social motivation and behavior. . . . The social group, the race or species, is the fundamental unit. The behavior of the individual can only be sane and effective when it is in alignment with this principle.

Burrow was a true explorer, a man of extraordinary gifts, a man of profound personal, as well as scientific, honesty. He was a passionate, dedicated student of human nature. He published about seventy scientific articles and six books. Until now, Burrow's findings and ideas have been largely lost to the behavioral scientists. The present volume is a revealing presentation of his thesis, and I am impressed by the pristine quality of the writing. The author marshals evidence, from many sources, of a fundamental unity within the organism of individual and group. Any member of the profession who wishes to study Burrow's works will be richly rewarded.

Certain questions arise in our present troubled situation. What is the specific "value twist" in our mechanized, power-oriented society that resists the truth in Burrow's discoveries? What forces in contemporary society oppose the acceptance of his main message?

Though it is surely useful to conjure up a vision of the ideal in health, a dream image of the potential achievements of human relations in a more favorable social matrix, this by itself is not enough. Regardless of the complexities and the dangers, too, we must find the way for human society to move from where it now stands, closer to where we would all like it to be. Throughout the years of his research, Trigant Burrow came to grips with this problem, and the steps he proposed for meeting it are worthy of serious consideration.

New York City   NATHAN W. ACKERMAN

EDITOR'S PREFACE

In the early years of his psychoanalytic work, Trigant Burrow introduced his concept of a primary strifeless phase of consciousness in the developing infant, which he called the "preconscious mode." As we know, Freud emphasized the conflict, hostility, and destructive emotional components prevalent in the parent–child relationship—incest for the parent of the opposite sex and Oedipal antagonism for the parent of the same sex. Burrow, on the other hand, stressed the presence of a harmonious mode of awareness and relationship in infant consciousness. He looked on this mode of consciousness as a direct reflection of the physiological continuity in life processes characterizing the organisms of mother and child during the infant's prenatal development. This physiological coordination with the mother is a universal experience of all human organisms and is, in Burrow's view, the biological substrate of the cohesive feelings and motivations which bind man to his fellows and to his physical world. This unitary phase is primary to consciousness and exerts a powerful influence on subsequent aspects of man's life.

It is Burrow's thesis that the primary identification of mother and child is developed earlier and is more basic than are the secondarily occurring conflicts and repressions that enter into this key relationship. His emphasis on this deeply positive and constructive element in man's consciousness and behavior anticipated the conceptions presented more recently by some exponents of existential psychiatry (Binswanger), as well as by such other writers as Erich Fromm, Ian Suttie, and members of the Washington School of Psychiatry.

The preconscious mode is, then, a mode of experiencing and feeling growing out of the infant's "primary identification with the mother." Writing years afterward of his recognition of this mode, Burrow said:

> This was the inception of a direction of thought and investigation with me of which all my later work has been the fuller development. There was no doubt with me that there existed between the infant and maternal organism a *tensional* rapport (I did not call it that at the time)—a total physiological continuity in sensation and reaction that underlay the entire developmental life of the organism and that was quite different from the tensional modifications brought about with the infant's adaptation to its environment *and to its mother* through the process of outer objective awareness (the employment of the symbol).[1]

Burrow first developed this concept in a paper he read before the New York Academy of Medicine in 1913.[2] During the next few years, other papers followed in which he applied his concept to such important psychoanalytic problems as homosexuality and incest.[3] He also accumulated an extensive file of material exemplifying symbolically this "phase of organic sensation and awareness"—material from the dream lives of his patients; from literature; from man's reactions to nature, to religion, to music, and to the mysterious; from the spontaneous responses of children and of primitive man.

But, although he had tentatively arranged the data in book form, Burrow felt constrained to set it aside.

> Something was incomplete. It did not satisfy me. I regretted this too, because I felt there was much material here of real interest to the investigator in the field of behavior. Still I waited. Then came the group investigation and the quite definite appreciation of the tensional continuity that

underlies not alone the processes of the individual in relation to its primary origin in the maternal organism, but that underlies also the processes of all individuals on the basis of their common physiological race origins.[4]

Speaking further of the extension of his early thesis, Burrow says:

In its original position this early principle of primary identification had significance merely as an accidental, isolated laboratory finding, and was limited in its application to the individual neurosis. As an isolated phenomenon it was, in its ontogenetic significance, necessarily applicable alone to an ontogenetic or individual basis of analysis. But . . . man is not an individual. His mentation is not individualistic. He is part of a societal continuum that is the outgrowth of a primary or racial continuum. . . . It is my thesis that this racial continuum is the phylogenetic basis of man's societal life precisely as the individual's early continuity with the maternal organism—his primary identification with the mother—is the ontogenetic basis for his subsequent development as an individual. . . .

In recent years the attempt has been made on the part of myself and a few students to establish a means for the practical recognition among us as individual organisms of this common substrate of feeling and reaction first posited theoretically under the symbol of the preconscious. Regarding this preconscious principle as the phyletic basis of individual mentation, it has been our practical endeavor to relate individual manifestations to this common racial principle shared among us. . . .[5]

As Burrow emphasized:

[T]he preconscious mood . . . is a common experience that finds expression in all the various phases of man's activities—in the distorted dreams and symbols of the neurotic and psychotic as well as in the creative productions of the poet, artist and scholar. But, in whatever form, it stems essentially from the basic organic unity that is the phyletic inheritance of man.

Many of the examples to be given represent the attempt of the neurotic, albeit symbolic and distorted, to achieve "peace" and a "home" through regression to that first home of abiding peace—the mother's womb. Unable to accept as essential reality the conflict, hostility, and aggression of "normal" behavior, the neurotic can offer only the groping and unconscious response of a baffled organism. But, however sick and disordered his symbolic, symptomatic responses, they are an earnest of the cohesive and inclusive bonds at the very source of man's consciousness and behavior—bonds which provide a solid foundation for the development of consciousness on a social and phyletic basis.

Through the years, the demands of more immediate and pressing work prevented Burrow from the full and leisurely development of his thesis of the preconscious and its thorough integration with his later findings. Though he devoted a chapter to the subject in *The Biology of Human Conflict*,[6] this summary statement represents a drastic condensation of the material.

Knowing Burrow's interest in turning his hand to the fuller presentation, I have attempted to carry this project forward as best I could. In doing so, I have been guided by the thought that it will have significance for artists and laymen as well as for students concerned with the creative aspects of behavior and for those interested in the psychoanalytic observations that formed the background of Burrow's pioneer researches. Needless to say, the volume would have been very different had Burrow lived to plan its final form and to see it through to completion. Although the nucleus of Burrow's thought developed consistently through the years, certain concepts presented in the early part of this book were later revaluated on the basis of his phylobiological researches. For example, he set aside the conventional acceptance of the neurosis as an individual expression, and he later regarded it as but a symptom of what he called "the social neurosis." Likewise, such distinctions in the study of behavior as "normal" and "neurotic" took on a changed significance for him. And the term "physiological" came to have a far more specific meaning as Burrow arrived at his finding of the relation of neuromuscular patterns to man's process of attention.

In the preparation of this volume, I have used much of Burrow's unpublished material dealing with this topic and have at times cut and rearranged it. In order to have the thesis complete, I have also made use of one of his early papers, "The Origin of the Incest-Awe,"[7] as well as parts of Chapter IV of *The Biology of Human Conflict*, which are distributed throughout the present book. Some illustrations of the preconscious mode as it is expressed in more recent literature have been added. Chapters 7, 8, and 9 have been organized and partly written by the editor, using Burrow's material wherever feasible. The editor, alone, therefore, must shoulder the responsibility for any weaknesses in these chapters, as well as for any failure in the integration of the material as a whole.

The Lifwynn Foundation   WILLIAM E. GALT
Westport, Connecticut

•

At the time Dr. Galt wrote the foregoing, he was chairman of the Editorial Committee of The Lifwynn Foundation. He was deeply interested, not only in the present book, but also in preparing a volume of Burrow's selected letters. His sudden death in 1955 at the age of fifty cut short his work on both these volumes, as well as on the many other projects he had in progress and which he looked forward to carrying out. In the absence of so dynamic and beloved a co-worker, those of us who remained have been slow to advance the ventures with which he was concerned. We turned first to the book of Burrow's letters with biographical notes which appeared in 1958 under the title, *A Search for Man's Sanity*.[8] But the present small volume had to be postponed more than once in favor of other pressing obligations.

With the exception of one small paragraph, nothing has been added to the manuscript since my husband completed his editing of it. The Editorial Committee has been concerned with shortening and tightening it—work which he had planned to do himself. The only liberty we have taken was to combine in a single chapter (Chapter 4) parts of two papers which Dr. Galt had included in their entirety as separate chapters.

In completing this undertaking, our committee was greatly heartened by the generous response of Nathan W. Ackerman, M.D., chairman of The Family Institute, whose views on the manuscript we invited. We deeply appreciated his sympathetic study of the material and the constructive tenor of his comments. Later, at our request he was good enough to write the Foreword, and we are much indebted to him for his perceptive appraisal of Burrow's contributions and their relation to current trends in behavioral science.

We should like also to thank George W. Hiltebeitel for his thoughtful suggestions and John C. Burnham, Ph.D., for reading the manuscript. Dr. Galt planned to acknowledge particularly the contribution of Michael Sperber, who assisted him in the preparation of the manuscript during two summers and whose enthusiastic participation in the task meant much to him. Hans Syz, M.D., president of The Lifwynn Foundation, joins the members of the Editorial Committee—Aimée Guggenheimer, Alfreda P. Sill, Charles B. Thompson, M.D., and myself—in expressing gratitude for the cooperation we have received.

The Lifwynn Foundation   ALFREDA S. GALT, Chairman
                              The Editorial Committee

NOTES

1. Letter from Burrow to Mrs. W. F. Dummer, December 19, 1935; published in *A Search for Man's Sanity*, "The Selected Letters of Trigant Burrow" (New York: Oxford University Press, 1958), p. 312.
2. "Psychoanalysis and Life," unpublished.
3. Cf. J. T. MacCurdy, "The Primary Subjective Phase of Burrow," *Problems in Dynamic Psychology* (New York: The Macmillan Company, 1922), pp. 188–205; D. H. Lawrence, *Psychoanalysis and the Unconscious* (New York: Thomas Seltzer, 1921), pp. 21 f.
4. *A Search for Man's Sanity, loc. cit.*
5. "The Laboratory Method in Psychoanalysis, Its Inception and Development," *The American Journal of Psychiatry*, V (1926), 348 f.
6. (New York: The Macmillan Company, 1937), pp. 66–103.
7. *The Psychoanalytic Review*, V (1918), 243–254.
8. Editorial Committee of The Lifwynn Foundation, *A Search for Man's Sanity*, "The Selected Letters of Trigant Burrow" (New York: Oxford University Press, 1958).

set aside the conventional acceptance of the neurosis as an individual expression, and he later regarded it as but a symptom of what he called "the social neurosis." Likewise, such distinctions in the study of behavior as "normal" and "neurotic" took on a changed significance for him. And the term "physiological" came to have a far more specific meaning as Burrow arrived at his finding of the relation of neuromuscular patterns to man's process of attention.

In the preparation of this volume, I have used much of Burrow's unpublished material dealing with this topic and have at times cut and rearranged it. In order to have the thesis complete, I have also made use of one of his early papers, "The Origin of the Incest-Awe,"[7] as well as parts of Chapter IV of *The Biology of Human Conflict*, which are distributed throughout the present book. Some illustrations of the preconscious mode as it is expressed in more recent literature have been added. Chapters 7, 8, and 9 have been organized and partly written by the editor, using Burrow's material wherever feasible. The editor, alone, therefore, must shoulder the responsibility for any weaknesses in these chapters, as well as for any failure in the integration of the material as a whole.

The Lifwynn Foundation   WILLIAM E. GALT
Westport, Connecticut

•

At the time Dr. Galt wrote the foregoing, he was chairman of the Editorial Committee of The Lifwynn Foundation. He was deeply interested, not only in the present book, but also in preparing a volume of Burrow's selected letters. His sudden death in 1955 at the age of fifty cut short his work on both these volumes, as well as on the many other projects he had in progress and which he looked forward to carrying out. In the absence of so dynamic and beloved a co-worker, those of us who remained have been slow to advance the ventures with which he was concerned. We turned first to the book of Burrow's letters with biographical notes which appeared in 1958 under the title, *A Search for Man's Sanity*.[8] But the present small volume had to be postponed more than once in favor of other pressing obligations.

With the exception of one small paragraph, nothing has been added to the manuscript since my husband completed his editing of it. The Editorial Committee has been concerned with shortening and tightening it—work which he had planned to do himself. The only liberty we have taken was to combine in a single chapter (Chapter 4) parts of two papers which Dr. Galt had included in their entirety as separate chapters.

In completing this undertaking, our committee was greatly heartened by the generous response of Nathan W. Ackerman, M.D., chairman of The Family Institute, whose views on the manuscript we invited. We deeply appreciated his sympathetic study of the material and the constructive tenor of his comments. Later, at our request he was good enough to write the Foreword, and we are much indebted to him for his perceptive appraisal of Burrow's contributions and their relation to current trends in behavioral science.

We should like also to thank George W. Hiltebeitel for his thoughtful suggestions and John C. Burnham, Ph.D., for reading the manuscript. Dr. Galt planned to acknowledge particularly the contribution of Michael Sperber, who assisted him in the preparation of the manuscript during two summers and whose enthusiastic participation in the task meant much to him. Hans Syz, M.D., president of The Lifwynn Foundation, joins the members of the Editorial Committee—Aimée Guggenheimer, Alfreda P. Sill, Charles B. Thompson, M.D., and myself—in expressing gratitude for the cooperation we have received.

The Lifwynn Foundation ALFREDA S. GALT, Chairman
The Editorial Committee

CONTENTS

Preconscious Foundations
of Human Experience

1

Introduction
An Unreckoned
Element

When, during the first decades of the twentieth century, Freud's dynamic formulations were gaining overwhelming ascendancy in the study of behavior, it seemed that at last a basic explanation of the problem of neurosis and psychosis had been found. As a student of psychopathology, I could not fail to be stirred by this new approach and was one of the first in this country to ally myself with it.

But, in spite of the fact that psychoanalysis answered many heretofore baffling questions, its intrinsic premise did not always satisfy me. Those of us who applied Freud's method in individual analysis had no difficulty in substantiating his basic postulate of a conflict within the neurotic personality due to sexual repression. Yet this factor of denied desire, of repressed libido, however hospitable a latitude was given it in Freud's interpretation, did not appear to me the whole account of things. Though it seemed to explain much that had long been puzzling in the behavior of the neurotic personality, it seemed also to leave out of reckoning much that was equally significant.

The situation was not at first clear to me. The psychoanalytic conception of repressed libido as the sole element in neurotic disturbances failed, it seemed to me, to take account of evidences of another trend that was revealed in the analysis of various types of patient.

Moreover, on careful study of the frame of reference of Adler's individual psychology, it became apparent that it offers no essential divergence from that of Freud. Here it is the individual's striving for self-satisfaction through overcompensating for the difficulties of nature and establishing his power by dominating his social milieu. These compensative demands constitute his conflict and occasion the complex multiplicity of appearances represented in the symptoms of the patient's neurosis. But, once more, something has been overlooked. The trend I had noted in my patients was not covered by Adler's hypothesis any more than by Freud's, notwithstanding the unquestioned value of each as a contribution to the solution of certain long-obscure problems of the neurosis.

However vague in outline as yet, this unsuspected element was, in my experience, too striking to be ignored. Of primary significance to me was the observation that this unexplained trend was in no way related to a dichotomous principle of striving or not striving, of gaining or not gaining (*Lust–Unlust Prinzip*)[1]—any more than is the upward thrust of a young tree or the motion of an ocean wave. It seemed to be characterized by a quality entirely alien to our "normal" mode of thinking. Indeed, it is not unreasonable to suggest that, in viewing the neurosis as dynamic (striving)—as a conflict of the self to be settled through the satisfaction of the self—one exhibits precisely the bias of the "normal" interpretation. Thus, in explaining the neurosis on the basis of the normal aim of getting or not getting for oneself, one is already victim of a subjective bias of observation that inevitably beclouds the significance of the phenomena observed.

On the basis of my observations, there seemed demanded a broader approach than was offered by our habitual reckoning. In fact, it was later demonstrated in the laboratory analysis of social groups undertaken by my associates and me that our accustomed orientation represents no valid criterion for the interpretation of pathological states. These investigations revealed that the standards of behavior of the community and those of the neurotic do not differ essentially. That is, the community does not impose on the neurotic, as a sort of alien, a distasteful censorship which blocks his "biological trends." Analysis of community reactions indicated that society, too, is the victim of compulsive drives toward self-satisfaction. Indeed, the behavior of the community as a whole is guided by standards as shifting and arbitrary as those of the neurotic. In other words, the individual is always allowed his personal prerogative provided he is able to gain his own self-approval and sees to it that he is not found out.

But this system of standards is one with which the individual neurotic is thoroughly familiar and which, through long habituation he has successfully mastered. Looking at behavior from the accustomed point of view as a striving for or against—the divisive motivation of "for me" or "not for me" or, in the terms of Freud, the sphere of the ambivalent unconscious—the neurotic is not handicapped by ignorance of the art of deceiving himself and others, an art in which the normal individual is also by no means untutored.

But, as I have said, an explanation of human behavior based solely on the alternatives of getting or not getting, whether manifested individually or socially, appeared too simple. It fails to include all the elements composing human personality. In fact, hardly a beginning has been made if we are to include the factor in human reaction to which I have referred as something existing apart from the domain of incentives and activities represented in the individual's drive toward his own private interest.

In disclosing the element of a definite struggle within the embattled personality of the neurotic, the school of dynamic psychology opened new horizons to students of human behavior. This formulation of a psychic conflict, of an internal issue between opposed trends in the feelings or emotions of our patients, has undoubtedly provided a powerful impetus toward solving the riddle of the neurosis. One element of the personality seeks, another denies; one strives, and one obstructs; one asserts its need, but finds it unfulfilled. However, as we have seen, the supposition that a moral censor resides in the community conscience with which the patient is identified (superego) and that the patient's basic trends are in conflict with this conscience is not convincing. It is too easy. There simply is no community conscience in the sense of an unwelcome authority imposed on the patient. Sociologically as well as biologically, patient and community are continuous with each other. Both yield equally to the lure of self-advantage, depending on the rewards promised and the securities provided against the chance of discovery. Assuredly, there is a conflict at the root of neurotic disorders, but the two elements of that conflict, as envisaged by the psychologists of the dynamic school, did not appear to me sufficiently biological in basis or in scope.

One of the cornerstones of psychoanalysis is its emphasis on the role of "resistances," which, for the neurotic, offer a barrier to relinquishing unconscious fantasies and to accepting reality—a concept of unquestioned value in the treatment of the psychoneuroses. Presumably the healthy individual feels entirely secure in the satisfaction of sexual desires which the neurotic patient is impelled to repress. Or the patient's libido has perhaps become attached to some object so inappropriate that sexual expression is blocked; his fellows of the healthier community have allegedly outgrown such infantile drives. But an explanation seemed called for that was based on more solid ground than the presumed virtue of society.

I found this problem more and more absorbing. Resistances, yes—but resistances to what? What were the opposed elements in the relentless conflict of the neurosis? Gradually, our experiments with social groups yielded a clue. There was no evidence of an influence imposed from without on the elements composing society. Rather, there was every evidence of an all-pervading conflict within the human organism. Far from being a problem personal to the individual neurotic, it was revealed as a situation in which the species generally is implicated.

For some time before we began our experiments with groups, quite definite and easily distinguished characteristics of neurotic patients had aroused my interest. In their reactions there were manifested certain explicit and unchanging qualities. The type of thinking and feeling which is based on wishful fantasy could be observed in them, of course, but there was another element that apparently had no relation to this dichotomous sphere of motivation. The domain of motivation that attracted my attention was apparently unrelated to the realm of feeling that strives, that struggles, that contends. From the point of view of origin and function, the two domains of motivation did not make contact at any point.

The principle of behavior I had noted was distinguished by a certain pervading quiet, a certain internal calm and self-possession, or a certain authoritative integrity of function. It seemed apparent that this quality was an integral part of the organism, independent of characterological variations, that it partook of the intrinsic authority of the race. Moreover—and this seemed of special significance—it was not confined to the neurotic individual, but was merely more easily observed in him because of the contrast it offered to the agitated struggles in which he was daily embroiled. Consistent observation revealed that this more serene, self-contained domain of reaction exists in the presumably well-adjusted personality as well as in his neurotic fellows. This finding was consistent with the related observation that all the components of discord recognized in the neurotic personality can be found also in the normal individual. Moreover these components, whether manifest or not, actuate the normal community quite as fiercely and insistently as that type of personality we look on as discrepant and which we term neurotic.

But let us look more closely at this quiet, integral aspect of consciousness which I found to be an underlying quality in the mood of my patients. I should like first to present the concept as it developed in the early years of my analytic work and to sketch its influence in bringing about the altered view with which I came to look on the problem of the neurosis. Later, I shall present evidence from other sources illustrative of the mood I first observed in my patients. In the final chapters, I shall attempt to correlate these early intimations with my thesis as it developed in its mature phases.

NOTE

1. Sigmund Freud, "Formulierungen über die zwei Principien des psychischen Geschehens," *Jahrbuch für Psychoanalytische und Psychopathologische Forschungen,* III (1912), 1–8.

The Principle of Primary Identification

2

The Strifeless Phase
of Awareness

The psychology of Freud is identical with the psychology of the unconscious, and the unconscious is identical with the sphere of repression or of sexual inhibition. The state of consciousness or the sensation we know as "sexual" is familiar to us all. We have studied its protean manifestations in the various records of human thought and human activity. We have seen its expressions in ourselves and in others, whether existing overtly or under the symbolic guise of repression. As such, its character is unmistakable. But just what it is—just what the specific nature of the state of consciousness that comes to our experience as sexual is—we have yet to determine. In chapters 3 and 4, I shall attempt to analyze it in greater detail.

As already indicated, I was equally impressed by a quite different mode of behavior in my patients—a mode of behavior not to be readily explained on the basis of sexuality and repression. I found intimations of human feeling or sentiment which appeared to relate to and reflect the primary physiological unity of the organism in its earliest moments of sentient experience. From these intimations, I was led to regard the infant's primary phase of consciousness—a phase I shall call the "preconscious"*—as one of complete identification with the mother.

I came to see that at first the mother was by no means the infant's love-*object*, but rather, if I may so express it, its love-*subject*. Lacking as yet the faculty of symbolic projection to be acquired only with later development and training, the infant organism does not, at first, look out toward or feel itself in objective relation to the mother. It does not *note mentally;* that is, it does not give a name or symbol to the presence it senses physiologically as the mother's organism.

Just as the infant is originally united physiologically with the mother, its body a continuous organism with her body, its self a part of her self, so in the infant's earliest stirrings of consciousness, its sensation and awareness remain still in subjective identification with the maternal organism. The child and the maternal organism are coterminous. There is no sense of separation, of distinction, of otherness. For the infant, there is at first no interval, no distance which must be bridged in order to reach the object opposite it, outside itself. As yet there exists no object, no opposite, no other self, nor aught outside itself. The organized whole embodied in the infant's preconscious behavior mode does not reflect only the primary physiological continuity between the organism of the newly developing infant and its biological matrix in the maternal organism. Also affirmed in this early mode of the infant's dawning awareness is the basic identity or consistency that united the organism's mental and physical spheres of behavior.

* Burrow's term "preconscious" must be differentiated from the psychoanalytic designation "preconscious," or "foreconscious," which means simply the aspect of mind that borders on consciousness.—ED.

In this primary subjective principle, there exists an element, or *prima materia*, that is of vital importance in the determination of the organism's ultimate adaptation to reality. This basic principle, or *prima materia,* is coterminous with the organism's internal pattern or posture as an organic whole, and through it the organism determines its relation to the external object as a whole. Although this principle of the organic whole must be carefully distinguished from the symbolic or projective mode of adult life, it is not without significance in the individual's later symbolic development. Whether in his total or in his symbolic relations, this subjective principle of reaction constitutes for the organism a central balance, an integral norm, through which it maintains throughout life its bionomic relation to the world of outer phenomena.

This intimation of a primary phase of consciousness in which the infant mind exists as a subjective extension, so to speak, of the mother's I called at the outset "the principle of primary identification." As we consider this primary mode of subjectivity that characterizes the preself, we find it to be a nonlibidinal, a preobjective, phase of the organism's development. On analysis, we also find that many subjective experiences occurring in the individual's later development indicate their close relationship to this primary preconscious phase of the organism. These experiences or modes of behavior contain no element of the competitive and contentious, no driving urge to get for oneself; they are not characterized by satisfaction, either in domination and aggression or in abject subordination and sentimental dependence. In the fleeting intimations of this later behavior, in which there is carried over into adult life the organism's primary mode of identification and unity, there is no opposite, no like and dislike, no "me" versus "you," no "right" and no "wrong." On the contrary, the sensations and reactions belonging to this mode intimate a subjectively quieter, more collected mood. They point to the presence of a more internally poised and self-possessed basis of adaptation than we ordinarily observe in the behavior reactions of either the normal or the psychoneurotic personality.

In illustration of this premental, preobjective mode, perhaps we shall find nothing more satisfactory than some lines from Romain Rolland's *Jean-Christophe* in which he attempts to reconstruct the infant's inner world of growing awareness. The novelist has described the amorphous stage of consciousness which I have called the preconscious in language which only the introverted, supersensitive, subjective artist mind could command. This deeply intuitive, imaginative passage is at the same time not lacking in fine clues to the organic implications in paranoia.

The day is immense, inscrutable, marking the even beat of light and darkness, and the beat of the life of the torpid creature dreaming in the depths of his cradle—his imperious needs, sorrowful or glad—so regular that the night and the day which bring them seem by them to be brought about.

The pendulum of life moves heavily, and in its slow beat the whole creature seems to be absorbed. The rest is no more than dreams, snatches of dreams, formless and swarming, and dust of atoms dancing aimlessly, a dizzy whirl passing, and bringing laughter or horror. Outcry, moving shadows, grinning shapes, sorrows, terrors, laughter, dreams, dreams. . . . All is a dream, both day and night. . . . And in such chaos the light of friendly eyes that smile upon him, the flood of joy that surges through his body from his mother's body, from her breasts filled with milk—the force that is in him, the immense, unconscious force gathering in him, the turbulent ocean roaring in the narrow prison of the child's body. For eyes that could see into it there would be revealed whole worlds half buried in the darkness, nebulae taking shape, a universe in the making. His being is limitless. He is all that there is. . . .

Months pass. . . . Islands of memory begin to rise above the river of his life. At first they are little uncharted islands, rocks just peeping above the surface of the waters. Round-about them and behind in the twilight of the dawn stretches the great untroubled sheet of water; then new islands, touched to gold by the sun.

So from the abyss of the soul there emerge shapes definite, and scenes of a strange clarity. In the boundless day which dawns once more, ever the same, with its great monotonous beat, there begins to show forth the round of days, hand in hand, and some of their forms are smiling, others sad. But ever the links of the chain are broken, and memories are linked together above weeks and months. . . . *

The rudiments, then, of the mental life lie in the organic reactions of the unborn child. At first merely vegetative, later physiological, there develops within the embryo a synthesis of function which we may call the primary, organic life. Here, in this preconscious mode, is embodied a phase of development in which the organism is at one with its surrounding medium. Here primitive consciousness is in a state of perfect poise, of stable equilibrium. Here, at its biological source within the maternal envelope, this organic consciousness is so harmoni-ously adapted to its environment as to constitute a perfect continuum with it.[1]

Such is the complete, all-sufficing, organic unity in the ex-periential life of the infant *in utero.* He wants nothing; his world is complete. But, with birth, the situation changes. The pleasant epoch of dreamless sleep is abruptly terminated. There no longer exist the fluid continuity and fulfillment that characterized the life of the organism during the months of its repose within the protecting membranes of the womb. With the infant's forcible expulsion from the paradise of peace and

* Translated by Gilbert Cannan (New York: Henry Holt & Co., 1915), I, 11 f. Copyright 1910; copyright renewed 1938 by Holt, Rinehart and Winston, Inc. Reprinted with permission of Holt, Rinehart and Winston, Inc., New York; Albin Michel, Paris; and William Heinemann, Ltd., London.—ED.

plenty, he enters a totally different world of experience.[*] Into the original, simple, unitary, homogeneous matrix of organic consciousness there now enter those gradual deposits of extraneous experiences caused by the organism's enforced adaptation to the external world, and these experiences constitute the nuclei of adult consciousness. The child has now entered a world of stubborn solidarity and can maintain life in consistent comfort and security only on a basis of relative

---

[*] This break in physiological continuity is graphically described by D. H. Lawrence in *Psychoanalysis and the Unconscious,* in which he refers to Burrow's early findings.

> There at the navel, the first rupture has taken place, the first break in continuity. There is the scar of dehiscence, scar at once of our pain and splendor of individuality. Here is the mark of our isolation in the universe, stigma and seal of our free, perfect singleness. Hence the lotus of the navel. Hence the mystic contemplation of the navel. It is the upper mind losing itself in the lower first-mind, that which is last in consciousness reverting to that which is first.
>
> A mother will realize better than a philosopher. She knows the rupture which has finally separated her child into its own single, free existence. She knows the strange, sensitive rose of the navel: how it quivers conscious; all its pain, its want for the old connection; all its joy and chuckling exultation in sheer organic singleness and individual liberty.
>
> The powerful, active psychic center in a new child is the great solar plexus of the sympathetic system. From this center the child is drawn to the mother again, crying, to heal the new wound, to re-establish the old oneness. This center directs the little mouth which, blind and anticipatory, seeks the breast. How could it find the breast, blind and mindless little mouth? But it needs no eyes nor mind. From the great first-mind of the abdomen it moves direct, with an anterior knowledge almost like magnetic propulsion, as if the little mouth were drawn or propelled to the maternal breast by vital magnetism, whose center of directive control lies in the solar plexus.
>
> In a measure, this taking of the breast reinstates the old connection with the parent body. It is a strange sinking back to the old unison, the old organic continuum—a recovery of the pre-natal state.

(New York: Thomas Seltzer, 1921), p. 51; reprinted with permission of The Viking Press, New York, and William H. Heinemann, Ltd., London; acknowledgment is made to Laurence Pollinger, Ltd., London, and the estate of the late Mrs. Frieda Lawrence.—ED.

adaptation to outer circumstance. Where formerly the psyche was in complete harmony with the enveloping medium, necessities of adjustment now arise that demand concession and sacrifice. It is only when the infant nourishes at the mother's breast that he experiences a semblance of organic unity, completion, and satisfaction.

Expressions of the larval mode of consciousness are to be found in certain dreams and experiences, examples of which will be presented briefly. But first let us remind ourselves of an important consideration. Though the element of conflict and its corresponding symptomatology undoubtedly loom large throughout the social activities of man, it must not be thought that all signs and symptoms are signs and symptoms of disease. Symptoms may be indicative of health and coordination as well as of discord and conflict. In a child, the emotional symptoms with which he responds to a natural fear-producing situation, such as the presence of an angry animal, are healthy indications of the organism's behavior reactions and possess a definite survival value; yet the same response to an innocuous social situation in a fear-conditioned adult is symptomatic of a definite behavior maladjustment that produces only a destructive, inhibiting effect. Similarly, an outer appearance, sign, or symptom may in one instance be indicative of the organism's sanity or wholeness, whereas in another the same manifestation may be definitely pathognomonic. Though the mimicries and dramatizations of hysteria are marks of a psychopathic trend, the tendency to masque and make-believe that characterizes primitive people and prompts the play of children is a symptom indicative of a wholesome developmental phase in the organism's ultimate adaptation to reality.

In the contrasting examples that follow—consisting of two dreams, the first that of a precoid and the second that of a manic-depressive patient—we have a similar situation in that each of the dreams is subject to two distinct interpretations. This discrimination becomes possible if—instead of approaching the dream merely from the viewpoint of the dissociative symbol, or metonymy, of the isolated individual—one approaches it from the viewpoint of *both* the symbolic, esoteric appearance and the total organic reaction. That is, the organism's recourse to metaphor—whether the private charade, symptom, or dream—is but the individualistic and restricted aspect of a symptomatology that reflects equally the far more constructive, integrative trend of the organism's total reaction. So, too, the dreams described below illustrate the merely private, esoteric charade represented in the truant reaction of conflict which is but the restricted and far-too-often misinforming aspect of the dream or symptom as a whole.

> I was in a cave. There was a faint light. It was very quiet and very restful. I was swimming and floating in a pool of water. The pool was very deep. It was all unusually beautiful. As I turned again to swim, my foot somehow touched bottom. It was muddy. I awoke with a start. But the quiet mood of the dream persisted.

> In my dream, there was a great fire which covered a large area or plot of ground. It seemed to me that the fire was so immense that it was burning everything between New York and Philadelphia. My mother was with me, and I was using every effort to get away from the fire. I felt that, if we would get to the ocean where we could find water, we would escape. We took a train and started on our journey. The fire seemed to be increasing, and we had a terrible time getting away from it. I could see everything burning and had a narrow escape from the limb of a tree which was on fire. We finally left the train and started up an alley or narrow street. My mother was following me. At the end of the alley, I found the ocean.

I am, of course, aware that, in the vulgate of psychoanalysis, the latter dream is of that typical class that illustrates conspicuously the dreamer's unconscious sexual appetency in respect to the mother. So it does. But does it follow by reason of the magnitude and importance of this discovery in the field of psychology or of man's outer symptomatology that the possibilities of inquiry are thereby exhausted? May we not ask if perchance anything else remains to be discovered on the still-uncharted seas of man's intraconscious, proprioceptive experience?

In both these dreams, there is, of course, the element of conflict as symbolized by the mud and the fire (the element that constitutes the characteristic basis of the psychoanalytic interpretation); but there is also the element of confluence and of unity as symbolized in the pool and the ocean, in the return to the medium of limitless waters, to the all-embracing sea, to mother earth, the great comforter, the home and the nest. This unitary element would seem to reflect the organism's predifferentiated, premental, or preconscious mode—the generic, prenatal mode of identification between the mother-organism and its offspring. There is the possibility that both the dreams derive their predominant significance from this primary, generic element of the preconscious, the larval instinct of the nest. From this viewpoint, it is not difficult to recognize that the significance of conflict in these dreams is quite secondary nor to trace the relation of this conflict to those acquisitive, unconscious elements that inhere in our present social-image interchange.

There are undoubtedly many instances in which there may be seen the apposition of the symbolism expressing the presexual mode with a frankly sexual symbolism. Throughout ecclesiastical ritual and ceremonial, for example, one finds conspicuously present this notable liaison between symbols that betray their markedly sexual motivation and symbols which are motivated in the greater quiet and serenity of the preconscious mode.

A schizophrenic patient during a delusional episode believed himself to be in the womb—the womb of his mother or of his sweetheart. He thought the reason that he was in the womb and that the doctors were observing him was that he had never had intercourse. Observe this juxtaposition of sex with the nest instinct.

This patient also fancied that he was a kind of atom or bubble or part of the solution in a pail of water and that he was passing into another world, that he came up through the ground—mother earth. Subsequently in his analysis, he submitted this dream:

> I was on the front porch at home. A very small spider came up, and it became larger and developed a large bulb on each side, and they got larger and larger, and the legs became large and hairy until it was a foot and a half high. It then attacked me, and I ran toward the door, and mother was just inside the door holding the door open for me. I believe I got in.

This dream shows again the conflict between the excitement and sexualization of the unconscious as against the quiet resolution of the preconscious mode.*

As further examples, I should like to submit two dreams related quite informally by a member of a social gathering one night in Zurich. All the men present belonged to professional and business ranks, and none were at all acquainted with psychoanalysis. The man who related the dreams happened to be a divinity student from Boston. The following day, I wrote and asked him to set down the two dreams for me, using as far

---

* Compare the following dream presented by Nandor Fodor, in which the dreamer was conscious of the uterine setting of the dream fantasy.

I was inside the Earth, yet at the same time I was conscious of being inside the uterus. It was round and I was watching the formation of the world. Things were in motion and the beauty of it was poignant. It was something you could not see at any other place. In the end I said: "If I stay here a little longer and watch, the timbers will crash down and I won't be able to get out. Then I got out of the cave."

"Varieties of Nostalgia," *The Psychoanalytic Review*, 37 (1950), 33.—ED.

as possible the same words as the night before. I might add that I was unacquainted with this man until the night of our meeting. Some years later, on reviewing these dreams, I was struck by the illustration they seemed to offer of the principle of primary identification and the inherence of the trends which we shall consider in chapters 3 and 4 as the underlying psychology of the neuroses. The first dream he called "The Disease-Germ Dream."

I felt myself bound hand and foot on a wide, rolling plain. Still, it seemed as though my head were an ancient castle and my ear the gate thereto, while I was walking to and fro on the wall above the gate as a warder on the watch. Presently I heard in the distance a mighty rumbling noise as if a great flood were approaching, and, as I looked intently across the plain, I saw coming up what seemed to be a black cloud which, on nearer approach, resolved itself into a vast host of armed knights, each mounted on a black charger and bearing a lance at rest, on which a pennant fluttered in the wind. There seemed to be millions of them, and the thunder of the horses was tremendous. I also saw the sunlight flashing from their polished armor. The host moved toward me with military precision and, just before the gate, halted. Then sixteen heralds mounted on snow-white horses rode out from the host, each bearing a silver trumpet to which was attached a banner of cloth of gold with heraldic device. They sounded a fanfare, and I challenged them from the wall above my ear, asking who they were, and they replied with thunderous voice "DISEASE GERMS," whereupon the great host marched into my ear and disappeared. I was struggling all the while to prevent this unwelcome intrusion and in doing so awoke. I was in a cold perspiration and trembling with fear.

The element of heightened subjectivity or homosexual symbolism here requires no comment.

I asked the dreamer to suggest what past impressions contributed to the dream, and he mentioned the following:

The notion of being bound on a vast plain is from Gulliver; the symbolism of the knights, from Mark Twain's *The Prince and The Pauper;* the approaching noise, etc., also from Mark Twain's impressions recorded in *A Tramp Abroad,* in which he describes the noise made by a mouse in the casement during a sleepless night. We who live in Boston, in what Chesterton has called the most degrading of atmospheres—a medical atmosphere—hardly require any explanation of the reference to germs.

The second dream was called the "Muscle Dream."

This was a horrible and degrading impression. I seemed to be wrapped from head to foot in a powerful muscle. The thing was alive and covered with blood. I distinctly felt its animal heat, and the slippery thing evaded my grasp. Its touch seemed to pollute my whole body and to fill me with loathing, but every effort to dislodge it only increased its tension. Slowly but surely, the thing seemed to be crushing the life out of me—but my chief concern was not of dying, but of dying in this fashion. It seemed to me that such a death would be disgraceful; and, as I struggled to get rid of the hot, polluting thing, I woke up. I was terribly afraid; every nerve in my body was quivering with excitement, and the whole room seemed filled with a nameless horror. I do not think I slept for hours after, so terrible was the impression. I have never been able to trace it to any past impression, nor can I account for it. It was distinctly the most horrible dream I ever experienced.

A clearer instance of a dream of *Mutterleibsphantasie* could hardly be imagined. From the viewpoint of the psychopathologist, it is obvious that the trend of this dream is one of regression and that it involves conflict in the emotional field. But it is equally obvious that the same dream, when viewed from the position of inherent continuity posited in the principle of primary identification, reflects an attempt on the part of the organism—though on a mental or symbolic level—to regain a basically unified feeling-mode. As I shall try to show in Chapter

3, it is precisely where the factor of the unconscious or the divisive sexual striving projects or regresses furthest toward the primary mother–child continuity—the sphere of the unified preconscious—threatening to invade the slumbering tranquility of the nest instinct, that there arises the most tumultuous conflict within the psyche. In its acutest phase, this conflict entails the cataclysm of the personality represented in dementia praecox or schizophrenia.

An incident in Jean-Jacques Rousseau's *Confessions* shows this conflict at the acme of its intensity. He relates that, when in the act of lifting a small table leaf, there set in those symptoms which later became the characteristic system of neurotic reactions dominating Rousseau's entire life. From the lexicon of dream symbols, as well as from the psychological context here, I cannot but infer that the table represents the mother and that the leaf symbolizes her skirt. Because of the interest of this incident in relation to the psychopathology of Rousseau, this passage may well be quoted in full.

At this time an accident happened, as singular in itself as in its subsequent consequences, which can only terminate with my existence.

One morning, being no worse than usual, while putting up a leaf of a small table, I felt a sudden and almost inconceivable revolution throughout my whole frame. I know not how to describe it better than as a kind of tempest, which suddenly rose in my blood, and spread in a moment over every part of my body. My arteries began beating so violently that I not only felt their motion but even heard it,[2] particularly that of the carotids, attended by a loud noise in my ears, which was of three or, rather four, distinct kinds. For instance, first a grave hollow buzzing; then a more distinct murmur, like the running of water; then an extremely sharp hissing, attended by the beating I before mentioned, and whose throbs I could easily count, without feeling my pulse, or putting a hand to any part of my body. This internal tumult was so violent that it has injured my auricular organs, and rendered me, from that time, not entirely deaf, but hard of hearing.

My surprise and fear may easily be conceived; imagining it was the stroke of death, I went to bed, and the physician being sent for, trembling with apprehension, I related my case, judging it past all cure. . . .

Till now, I had been a great sleeper, but a total deprivation of repose, with other alarming symptoms which have accompanied it, even to this time, persuaded me I had but a short time to live. This idea tranquillized me for a time. . . .

This accident, which seemed to threaten the dissolution of my body, only killed my passions, and I have reason to thank Heaven for the happy effect produced by it on my soul. I can truly say, I only began to live when I considered myself as entering the grave; for, estimating at their real value those things I was quitting, I began to employ myself on nobler objects, namely by anticipating those I hoped shortly to have the contemplation of, and which I had hitherto too much neglected. I had often made light of religion, but was never totally devoid of it; consequently, it cost me less pain to employ my thoughts on that subject, which is generally thought melancholy, though highly pleasing to those who make it an object of hope and consolation; Madame de Warens was more useful to me on this occasion than all the theologians in the world would have been.[3]

I think that this passage may well be given careful psychoanalytic study. The correspondence between the number and character of the sounds subjectively perceived by Rousseau and the number and character of the sounds stethoscopically perceptible in the pregnant mother as she approaches full term cannot, it seems to me, be lightly dismissed as a mere coincidence. Nor is it in the present case a valid objection that the subject had at some former time heard or read of these sound components which are now distinguishable on auscultation of the pregnant uterus, for, at the time this occurrence was recorded, these auditory sound phenomena were still unknown to obstetrics.[4] Observe that, with the occurrence of this episode, which I regard as derived from preconscious fantasy,

Rousseau records the simultaneous destruction of his sexual libido.

The circumstance of the onset of Rousseau's neurosis recalls a similar situation which marked the onset of a condition of anxiety hysteria in a former patient of mine. This incident, which likewise ushered in, with a sudden and terrible swoop, the overwhelming train of symptoms comprising the manifest content of this patient's neurosis, consisted of the sudden fancy which one day came to him as he raised his eyes momentarily to a statue of the Virgin. The fancy which seized him was the thought of raising the skirt and seeing the uncovered form of the "Mother of God." In this instant, there swept over him the first onrush of the unspoken horror that for years after clouded and oppressed the course of his life.

But I should like now to turn to the origin of such behavior expressions as it appeared to me early in my psychoanalytic practice.

NOTES

1. The reader is referred to Ferenczi's interesting contributions concerning the unconscious influence of the prenatal and early infantile experience on the subsequent life of the individual and particularly on the development of the sense of reality. According to Ferenczi, in the early developmental period of the growing human organism a gradual adjustment to reality establishes itself. The fetal stage, which is without wishes or wants, is followed by various "periods of omnipotence." As may be easily appreciated, Ferenczi's concept differs markedly from the concept of "the preconscious" as here presented. Sandor Ferenczi, "Entwicklungsstufen des Wirklichkeitssinnes," *Internationale Zeitschrift für ärtzliche Psychoanalyse*, I (1913), 124–138; *idem*, *Contributions to Psycho-analysis* (Boston: Richard G. Badger, 1916), Chapter VIII, "Stages in the Development of the Sense of Reality," pp. 181–203.

2. It is doubtful that this subjective experience resulted from the physiological response cited. On feeling a patient's pulse who alleged that he was at the moment experiencing a similar episode —rapid throbbing of the arteries, etc.—I found the pulse rate normal and the pattern entirely regular.

3. *The Confessions of Jean-Jacques Rousseau* (New York: Tudor Publishing Company, 1928), pp. 344–346.

4. The existence of these uterine sounds was clinically established in the early nineteenth century. See Joseph B. De Lee, *The Principles and Practice of Obstetrics* (Philadelphia: Saunders, 1938), pp. 300–303.

3

The Origin
of the Incest Awe

EROS

They put their finger on their lip,
The Powers above:
The seas their islands clip,
The moons in ocean dip,
They love, but name not love.

—EMERSON

If it were asked which of the manifold items unearthed by psychoanalysis has been shown to be the most important, the answer would be the mental revolt against the sexual implication of the primary relation of the infant to the maternal organism—the reaction recognized under the name of "incest awe" (*Inzest-Scheu*). Because of the basic significance of this factor in relation to disordered mental states, perhaps no subject can engage the interest of the psychopathologist with larger offers of reward than that of the genesis of the incest horror—the reaction technically known as the Oedipus complex.

Referring to this moral repugnance inherent in the idea of incest, W. G. Sumner says that "the ultimate causes of the law of incest . . . lie beyond our investigation."[1] I do not believe it. I do not believe that this biological phenomenon is beyond the range of comprehension. I believe that, if we will follow to their ultimate conclusion the genetic data of consciousness which have been made accessible through the dynamic psychology of Freud, we shall not only reach a solution of the innate repugnance represented by the incest awe, but we shall find that the solution of this phenomenon possesses an almost self-evident simplicity.

With regard to the problem of the incest revolt, certain students have been content to merely affix the generic label of "instinct" and there to let the matter rest. But, if the incest revolt is a problem that is pertinent to psychoanalysis, we cannot be satisfied with any such inclusive generality. To invoke the oceanic concept of biological instinct is inadequate to the criteria of psychoanalysis. Besides, if I understand the meaning of the term "instinctive," it refers to an inherent, integrative trend determining the specific reactions of organisms with reference to their species. Now, certainly the primary attachment of the child to the mother is instinctive. In referring to its characteristic manifestation, we show our agreement in speaking of "the instinct of suckling." If, then, the revolt due to the recognition of this primary fixation, or incest horror, is instinctive, we are driven to the conception of two elemental and inalienable instincts essentially opposed to each other— two genetic, cosmic impulses set at cross-purposes. Thus against an inherent urge of nature itself we erect a no less inherent counterurge.

At the furthest extreme from this biological position, there is the more widely accepted psychological explanation. According to this account, incest awe is due to the interdictions of society, to the universal ban of convention and of civilization. That is to say, the incest revolt is regarded as the individual's response to a general social prohibition. This position seems to me merely begging the question. To appeal to custom is to proceed from mouth to source. Such an account is certainly not genetic. Social custom is a derivative, not an elemental, factor. The dynamic and inherent process of organic law precedes the mere consideration of social bias. Indeed, to cite social proscription as the account of a reaction as biological and inherent as is incest awe is comparable to a process of reasoning which would ascribe to ecclesiastical ordinance the origin of the religious impulse. That an argument so superficial should have found adherents among us is of itself proof, it seems to me, of our remoteness from the true interpretation of this reaction, that is, from the genetic account of this phenomenon.

I cannot help feeling that the vicarious rationalizations which have been thus far accepted indicate that the psychoanalyst is here face to face with an almost insurmountable resistance within himself, that here is presented a crisis in the handling of which psychoanalysis has very nearly met its Waterloo. I cannot otherwise account for the general acceptance within the ranks of psychoanalysis of an explanation which is not only utterly inadequate from the point of view of logic, but which so entirely abrogates the sworn aims and methods of the psychoanalytic ideal.

I believe that we shall gain a distinct advantage in studying this problem if, as I suggested earlier, we separate our notions of what is primary, subjective, and biological from what is secondary, objective, and psychological—if we will separate our conception of unconscious biological *unity* from our conception of the conscious sexual *affinity*. In this process, we isolate from our concept of the conscious sexual life (the so-called unconscious, when subjected to repression) the concept of the *preconscious* mode of awareness, representing the original state of the infant psyche. With this distinction in view, let us for the moment leave the consideration of psychological mechanisms—the dynamic reactions with which psychoanalysis is concerned (reactions which, I feel more and more, are effects rather than primary causes)—and proceed to the study of this antecedent stage of consciousness.

As already emphasized, the relation between the mother and the suckling infant is primary and biological—the one perfect, complete phase of conjugation. Existing without object, it is, so to speak, one with life, like the course of the planets or the growth of trees. Being preconscious, it is in the truest sense unconscious.

This unity with the mother exists, however, only in respect to the affective sphere, to the primary feelings and instincts. That is, it belongs to the subjective life of the organism, for there is as yet no cognition, no objectivation, no contrasting of the ego with the outer world, of the self with other selves—no "consciousness," in the habitual sense.

As I have pointed out, the demands of the world of outer objectivity or of consciousness proper entail increasing inroads on this state of primary quiescence. More and more they disturb the organism's vegetative repose. Thus, our primary nature tends to shrink from the intrusion of those outer impressions which disturb its elemental sleep. Slowly, there is the establishment of that rapport between the organism and the external world which constitutes individual adaptation. Observe that the process of adaptation is essentially outward-tending, away from the ego, that it is inherently a process of *objectivation.*

With increasing objectivation, this outer rapport is later established in respect to the organism itself. Objectivation returns upon the very self from which it set out. The self becomes its own object, and consciousness is, as it were, infolded. Being thus turned in on itself, the organism has attained a state of mental development which distinguishes the human species from the rest of the animal world—the stage, namely, of self-consciousness.

As long as the consciousness of self, even though a process of infolding, remains within the mode of cognition, it is but the more inclusive process of objectivation, and self-consciousness proceeds smoothly and uniformly. Even though there is the recognition of the self in respect to conduct—the relating of the ego to the outer act—consciousness maintains a constant course as long as the process remains objective. The result is a uniform process of adaptation. But, when this cognitive function applies itself to the primary affective sphere, when this objective principle is turned in on an essentially subjective mode, an inherent discrepancy arises. The subjective and objective spheres being essentially opposite and unassimilable, there is here an attempt to unite opposed and mutually exclusive principles, an attempt to turn about on the essential self, to reconcile two phases of consciousness which are inherently incompatible.

This disparity between trends that pertain respectively to the subjective and the objective spheres of experience is illustrated on every hand. The difference lies in the fact that that which we *feel* (the subjective) flows from within out, whereas that which we *apprehend* (the objective) flows from without in. In the first is represented the immediacy of affectivity,* in the second, the circumvention of cognition, rationalization, reflection. The one expresses the world of feeling; the other, the world of thought.

My position is that these two components of consciousness are incompatible. Pure cognition or reason impairs the processes of pure affective perception, and vice versa. The essence of the affect of enjoyment is its spontaneity. One yields oneself completely to it; one does so, that is, nonconsciously. Conversely, experience is robbed of enjoyment, of its affective

---

* Burrow used the word "affectivity" here as synonymous with the organism's primary feeling. Later he differentiated between primary, total feeling and "affect," or feeling that has been distorted by the inclusion of a projective, cognitive, or symbolic element.—ED.

quality, when it is too consciously, too objectively, encountered. In the presence of beauty, one is caught up by the feeling it invites and forgets to think. When asked to think about it, one is, as we say, "brought down to earth again," that is, he has left the realm of feeling and encountered again the world of "hard" fact.[2] It is so with music, with painting, with poetry, with all forms of art appreciation, such appreciation being a process of feeling, sympathy, *identification*. If this is true of affective appreciation in respect to art, to nature, to the harmonious elements about us, how much more is it true of the harmonious principles within ourselves, of those organically subjective states of experience which we know as the reactions of love.

Love is unity, participation, understanding. It is simple, harmonious, unquestioning. Love is one with life itself. It is life in its subjective relation. Cognition, on the contrary, pertains to contrast, demarcation, distinction. It is close kin to pride. In other words, it is synonymous with acquisition, aim, calculation. Hence it is kin to self-interest, to desire, that is to say, to *sex*.*

It is my thesis that the irreconcilable mental conflict represented in the incest revolt is the expression of the inherent discrepancy due to this reversal of life when the objective mental principle is turned in on the essentially primary, subjective phase of consciousness. It is the conflict embodied in the opposition between love as aspiration and life, on the one hand, and sexuality as covetousness and self, on the other. Thus, in my interpretation, incest awe is the subjective reaction resulting from an affront to an inherent psychobiological prin-

---

* Since Burrow later used the word "sexuality" instead of "sex" to denote the divisive, acquisitive, and self-reflective response, the word "sexuality" has been substituted in the following paragraphs. Compare Chapter VIII of *The Social Basis of Consciousness*, in which he contrasts the "suggestive, substitutive image-systematization of sexuality" with "the unification and spontaneity of sex."—ED.

ciple of unity. It is the revulsion due to the impact of an organic contradiction.

Love is without object. It is whole, spontaneous, free. Sexuality has its object, its divisive gratifications. Sexuality always clashes with love. It is self, and love is precisely the unawareness of self. As Nietzsche says, "There are moments, spoken from the clear fire of love, in whose light we understand the word 'I' no longer."

It is, then, precisely where there is love in fullest measure that we should expect the strongest repudiation of the sexual mode. And this complete realization of love is surely to be found in the relation of mother and offspring, a manifestation of love that is primary, organic, and biological. It is here that we should expect the most profound recoil of the human spirit from the instigations of sex. It is in respect to the mother—to the family where there exists that unpremeditated affection we call love—that we naturally find the strongest conflict with sex.

Such, I maintain, is the meaning of the horor of the incest revolt. I contend that incest awe is unthinkable except as the objective consciousness of an inherently subjective mode of experience, that incest is the mind's recoil at the rending in twain of what was before biologically simple and indissoluble —the primary, homogeneous, subjective ego. Thus, there is no incest but thinking makes it so. Nature will not tolerate the encroachment of consciousness in the sphere of that primary, affective preconscious which pertains to the original subjective unity and identity of the organism with the maternal life source.

In this view, then, the incest revolt is the shock due to the impact of consciousness on its inherent self. This is the meaning of sexuality. This is the meaning of repression. This is the meaning of sin. Sin consists, not in nakedness, but in the knowledge of nakedness, not in the genital organ, but in the fig leaf with which it is concealed. It is to *behold* our nakedness. It is to objectify and render conscious an inherently preconscious, subjective state of being. This is why sex is "impure." Convention does not make it so. It is of itself impure; that is, it is not simple, not unmixed, not unalloyed.[3] I repeat, incest is not forbidden; it forbids itself. It is the protest of our organic morality. Its prohibition is inherent. It is primary and biological.

Let us look at the testimony of the folk unconscious, as recorded in history, in literature, in religion, and in language. The Biblical usage, "to know a woman," means to have sexual intercourse with her, and there is the legal term "to have carnal knowledge of a woman." Moreover, it is the highest commendation of virtue to say that a person is "innocent." In legal parlance, this word means "not guilty," but, if we inquire into the real implication of the term, we find that what is actually conveyed by it is "lack of worldly knowledge." That is, we are identifying virtue with ignorance, knowledge with sin.

No better proof of the psychobiological identity of knowledge and sin is to be found than in the sources of philology. Through a comparative study of language, we find that the word "sin" is related to the Anglo-Saxon *soth*, which means "sooth" or "truth," and to the Gothic word *sunja* which also means "truth." Similarly, a comparison with the Latin and Icelandic forms reveals an etymological kinship between words which mean "being" or "being so" and our English word "sin." Thus we see that the psychobiological theory which relates sin to knowledge is actually substantiated by the records of man's earliest forms of expression.*

---

* There are also other words that indicate the strong association in the folk mind between the concepts of knowledge and sin. For example, the word "cunning" comes from the same root as knowledge, and "shrewd" which comes from the Middle English *schrewen*, "to curse," has had such diverse meanings as "bad," "evil," "knowing," and "sagacious." In addition to its present signification of "arrogance" or "self-centeredness," the word "conceit" has the archaic meaning of "thought," "thinking," or "knowledge." Then there is our word "wise" that carries the

Consider, too, how all *knowledge* has had to struggle for advance against the universal prejudice of "sin," how from Pliny and Galileo to Darwin and Freud the progress of knowledge has had to contend against a superstitious implication of evil. The outcry against the "knowledge" introduced by Freud has been the more violent by reason of the direct outrage to the subjective ego occasioned by his investigations—investigations which force the primary mind from its pleasant immanence of quiescent unconsciousness into the boldly disruptive actuality of consciousness. But why this ban on knowledge? Because knowledge is sin. Because through knowledge is begotten the *realization* of those organic reactions which constitute sex.

The fall of man consisted in his having eaten of the tree of the *knowledge* of good and evil. Here, again, knowledge is sin. This is what is meant by man's "original sin." Thus, again, the folk mind records in unmistakable symbols its intuitive realization of the inherent sin of knowledge. If we will read between the lines of the Book of Genesis the thoughts that underlie the manifest content of this symbolic legend, we cannot fail to see the identity between the idea of sexuality and the objectivation of the primary consciousness. "And the Lord God commanded the man, saying, Of every tree of the garden thou mayest freely eat. But of the tree of the knowledge of good and evil thou

---

sinister meaning of "cunning" or "crafty," as well as the meaning "intelligent" and "learned." Compare also the Scotch word "canny."

The Latin verb *mentiri* (*mens*, "mind") originally meant "to use the mind," and this meaning has survived in our word "mentation." Later, however, *mentiri* came to mean "to lie," a meaning which is preserved in the English word "mendacious." Spanish *hablar*, "to speak," is derived from the Latin *fabulare*, from which our word "fable" comes. Our word "crime" traces its etymology to the Latin *cernere*, "to think," Greek κρίνειν. Related words are "canny," "can," Scot. "knowledge" and "cunning," "keen," and "ken," from the Anglo-Saxon *cunnan*, "to know" (German *kennen*). See William E. Galt, "Our Mother Tongue—Etymological Implications of the Social Neurosis," *The Psychoanalytic Review*, 30, 1943, 241–262.—Ed.

shalt not eat of it . . ." (2:16–17). And again, in reference to Adam and Eve, we read: "And they were both naked, the man and his wife, and were not ashamed" (25). Later (3:7), relating the consequence of the disobedience of Adam and Eve, it is said that "the eyes of them both were opened, and they knew that they were naked; and they sewed fig leaves together, and made themselves aprons." Again (3:9–11): "And the Lord God called unto Adam, and said unto him, Where art thou? And he said, I heard thy voice in the garden, and I was afraid, because I was naked; and I hid myself. And he said, Who told thee that thou wast naked? Hast thou eaten of the tree, whereof I commanded thee that thou shouldest not eat?"

Similarities to the Hebrew tradition of the fall of man are to be found in Greek mythology. According to John A. Symonds, "the conscience of the Greeks and Jews, intent on solving the mystery of pain and death, convicted them alike of sin."[4] The gods impose a prohibition on just one thing, and there is an act of transgression precisely in regard to this one command. In the legend of Psyche and Eros, Psyche must never see Eros.[5] If she does, he will not return. She contrives to see him, and he is lost to her. So of Zeus and Semele. Semele is beloved of Zeus, but must never ask to see him in all his godlike glory. She does ask and is withered by the sight. In the story of Orpheus and Eurydice, Orpheus can bring Eurydice back to life if, leading her from Hades, he will refrain from turning to look at her. He turns and looks at her and loses her forever. Again, in Norse legend, Elsa must not ask the name of Lohengrin. She does so, and he must depart. There is a like motive in the story of Pandora's box, of Lot's wife, of Proserpine, and of others. In countless varieties of setting, the same theme, with its ever-recurring prohibition motive, is presented over and over again in the allegorical symbols of the racial unconscious.

That the folk mind should be imbued with so profound a conviction of sin as indicated by this general prohibition motive inherent in its earliest and most durable legends must indicate some deeply biological principle in human consciousness. It seems to me that this principle is nothing else than the innate abhorrence by the primary affective sphere of consciousness of the ruthless incursion of an alien objectivity.

From this source, I believe, has arisen the widespread perversion of the human spirit which has caused the hideous distortion of values embodied in the repressive subterfuge and untruth of our so-called moral codes and conventions. I cannot see the expressions embodied in these reactions of the social organism as other than vicarious representations of an organic law of life, as the feeble efforts of man's immature consciousness to compensate his essential nature for the frustration and denial of his inherent life. These distortions of life represent the organic outrage to this innate principle of unity occasioned by the enforced encroachment of conscious objectivation on his original, spontaneous subjectivity and oneness.

Thus, man's "morality"—the code of behavior that represents psychologically the zealously courted standard of conduct he designates "normality"—is, in my view, nothing else than an expression of the neurosis of the race. It is a complex of symptoms representing the hysterical compensations of society that are precisely analogous to the compensative reactions manifested in the hysteria of the individual. As "morality" is essentially the pain of the neurotic due to an intuitive sense of his inadequacy to the demands of his own code of behavior, so morality expresses equally the pain of the social organism because of its inaptitude to meet the requirements of the generic social code. The "hysteria" of the one is the "normality" of the other, but in both the inherent psychological mechanism is identical, the mechanism in the one as in the other representing vicarious compensations due to the frustration of principles of organic truth. So much for the morality representative of "normality."

Among the lower animals, there is no recognition of sexuality. There is no sin. There is no morality. They have not eaten of the tree of the knowledge of good and evil. That is, consciousness has not yet ousted them from their Eden of innocence, for the vital separation in the psyche through the birth of objective consciousness has not been imposed on them. It is this extraneous interpolation in the consciousness of man, this innovation causing a violation of the primary mind principle, or the essential preconscious, which I believe to be the psychological interpretation of the horror entailed in incest awe.

"Cursed is the ground for thy sake," said God to Adam.[6] This is the universal world tragedy; this is the conflict indigenous to the mental life; this is the doom under which man labors because of his attainment of the knowledge of good and evil. Such, in a word, is the curse of life embodied in the repressed, distorted reactions constitutive of sexuality and its disguised equivalents. Hence the parable which represents the first man as an outcast, a wanderer sent forth under a life sentence of hard labor to toil by the sweat of his brow and reap in the end a harvest of thorns and thistles. It is the allegory of the world's neurosis, the prodrome of that universal anguish popularly interpreted as life.

The psychoanalyst has ample opportunity to recognize the ban under which sexuality is represented as sin and the consequent repression of this sphere in order to deny it objective recognition in consciousness, for it is in the soul of the neurotic patient that this tragic conflict has entered most deeply and with most vital consequences.

We who study the riddle of the neuroses from day to day and from hour to hour have learned at least that these disorders are essentially exaggerated states of self-consciousness, that they are due to a confusion of the subjective and the objective spheres of mind. When we have penetrated to the innermost fastnesses of the disquieted minds of our patients, we find that this conflict is synonymous with the consciousness of sex and with the horror embodied in incest awe.

NOTES

1. *Folkways*, "A Study of the Sociological Importance of Usages, Manners, Customs, Mores, and Morals" (Boston: Ginn and Company, 1906), p. 482.
2. For example, see Rupert Brooke's poem, "The Voice," *The Collected Poems of Rupert Brooke* (New York: John Lane Co., 1916), p. 88.
3. It frequently happens that young men, possessed of the popular prejudice in favor of sexual functioning per se as a requisite test and verification of "manhood," find themselves inadequate to the act when favored with such opportunities as are conceded by the promiscuous type of women who render themselves available for such enterprise. A conflict is the outcome. There is apprehension in regard to their "potency," and they consult a doctor.

   I know that the popular view is in favor of sexual functioning as such, that in these cases it is customary to assume the existence of a pathological condition calling for immediate treatment— "treatment," whatever its method, having in aim the patient's encouragement to successful cohabitation.

   In the light of the conceptions this paper attempts to set forth, I am at variance with this whole tendency of interpretation. If such individuals are impotent to satisfy the sex demand presented in such commercial arrangements, they are, in my observation, by so much the more adequate to fulfill the requirements of the larger and deeper affiliations based on the permanent unions of love.

   Even so technically skilled a psychoanalyst as Ferenczi (*Contributions to Psycho-analysis* [Boston: Richard G. Badger, 1916], p. 19) and so faithful an adherent of Freud as he to the contrary notwithstanding, I cannot but feel that a psychoanalysis is of a very shallow and short-sighted order that fails to recognize, in this situation, on which side lies the alternative of health and on which that of pathology and that does not assist the more constructive, conservative, integrative process that is shown in the individual's instinctive repudiation of these dissociated and perfunctory trade arrangements. It seems to me that, in this instance, the perplexed youth is *biologically* truer to form than his professional consultant.

4. John A. Symonds, *Studies of the Greek Poets* (New York: Harper & Brothers, n.d.), p. 169.

5. See the charming narrative by Walter Pater in *Marius the Epicurean* (New York: Boni and Liveright, n.d.), pp. 50–75.

6. *Genesis* 3:17.

4

The Social Import
of the Preconscious

On grounds of practical significance, the preconscious, as I use the term, has its strongest claim to consideration in the fact that the recognition of this sphere was but a response to the urgency of trends actually embodied in the mode itself. In speaking of his conception of the unconscious, Freud well said that the unconscious was by no means his invention; it was the outcome of observations resulting of necessity from the objective witness of the evidence at hand.

In a sense, Freud had nothing to do with his concept of the unconscious. His relation to it was that of a solvent toward the reagents which enter into it. Said Freud, as it were: "Here are mental manifestations worthy of consideration," and the result was the unconscious. He merely allowed what *is* to *be*. In formulating his theory out of the objective materials furnished him in the related but as yet uncoordinated experience of his patients, Freud merely interpreted them to themselves.

That which Freud observed in his patients was a psychic conflict due to the presence in them of repressed sexual trends. But, in recognizing these trends as repressed or unconscious, Freud observed not only sexual trends but also a moral duress represented in the conflict under which these trends presented themselves. Accordingly, in Freud's interpretation, man is represented as primarily sexual, that is, as normally *craving* (libido) the attainment of sensual satisfaction per se. Any indifference or repugnance to such forms of satisfaction he regards as pathological, whereas whatever repose and self-containment the individual commands, as shown in the tendency to sexual continence, represents a mere conformity secondarily imposed by the dictates of an extraneous social order. The sexual libido or the pleasure-quest being in Freud's view the basis of conscious experience, sexuality or the craving of self-satisfaction is accordingly, in his conception, the primary and normal condition to be confronted in the study and adjustment of the problems of human behavior.

No unprejudiced investigator could for a moment doubt the validity of Freud's view of his complete consistency with respect to the observable data. But, as regards the *genesis* and the ultimate biological *meaning* of this conflict of the unconscious, as it bears on the origin of mental experience and therefore on the genetic and evolutionary interpretation of human consciousness, my own position is the direct reverse of Freud's.

According to my thesis, man is primarily, genetically nonsexual (using the term "sexual" in the accepted meaning of an inherent urge toward the satisfaction of physical sensations for their own sake).[1] In this view, the restless and obsessive acquisitiveness toward sensual satisfaction everywhere existing as "normal" and inherent is, on the contrary, a condition that is itself wholly induced by the universal repression incident to consciousness. Far from being the deterring influence to the urge of sexuality as Freud regards them, the superimposed interdictions and conventions of society are, in my conception, but the larger phase of this selfsame repression. And this repression is the essential meaning of what is popularly called "the sexual urge."

Repression, I repeat, is not a disorder of the isolated neurotic mind. It is a disorder of the common social mind. The difference is that the social mind has adopted a diplomatic attitude toward this factor of repression of which it is itself a victim. I think that this has not been generally recognized. I think that it has not been recognized that the repression of the social consciousness—through which are begotten those inhibitions we are wont to interpret as the abrogation of sexuality—is the factor wholly answerable for the restless obsessiveness of physical desire interpreted today as the sexual urge. It is the aim of this chapter to consider the social repression of which this so-called sexual urge is the outcome—an urge implicitly sponsored by psychoanalysis under the scientific formulation of the "sexual instinct."

A scientifically controlled attempt to study any phenomenon presupposes an absence of bias from the conditions of observation. If we are to study the inherent psychology of man, it is first necessary to secure conditions that will exclude prejudice toward our inquiry through the interference of the unconscious of man himself. Psychoanalysis is the laying-bare of one's own biases and contemplating them with impartial consideration. Hence, the whole position of psychoanalysis is based on the individual's voluntary submission to the conditions of a controlled experiment in which he himself is the subject. It is not otherwise with the study of the social mind. We cannot discover the inherent law of the collective consciousness until we have first reached a position of impartiality toward the social unconscious of which we are ourselves a part.

It is not easy to look dispassionately on an unconscious situation of which we ourselves are the sponsors. Violent resistances of our own immediately confront us, for an analysis of the social mind is an analysis of ourselves, and a self-analysis, as we know, is the most difficult and unwelcome of all tasks. In undertaking it, we cannot be too urgently forewarned against the tendency which will again and again appear in us in the form of resistances to the very inquiry on which we are entering, presumably with entire scientific impartiality.

It is needful to recognize that there is a complex of the social as well as of the individual mind and that, since we ourselves are a part of the social mind, a social complex is insofar our own complex. Leaving aside high-sounding terms, a complex is nothing more nor less than a simple, everyday prejudice. It is seeing a thing as we like to see it or are habituated to seeing it, rather than as our impartial judgment warrants. It is a point of view arising from motives of narrow personal gain, rather than from those of a broad, constructive purpose.

If we consider it, I think we shall find that nowhere does the human mind delight to indulge the whimsies of personal preference with more fatal consequences to reason than in those popular tendencies of the social consciousness manifested in what is known as its "beliefs." Beliefs are the habitual pacifiers of immature man. They are the outstanding biases of the social mind and, as such, are the major complex of the social consciousness. In the savage, they exist as superstition; in so-called civilized society, as religious dogma. In the formulations of our more progressive cultural spheres, they may even appear as "scientific hypotheses."[2] But, in each instance, one detects the calcification of ingrained prejudice, the habituated complex, the encrusted belief. In all these manifestations of the social mind, as of the individual consciousness, one observes the tendency to consolidation characteristic of the complex. There is the unconscious quest of a fixation point, a place of settlement, of conclusion, of finality. It is indeed significant that the man who has reached a belief expresses it by saying that he has "come to the conclusion." He has indeed, for, in the prejudice of belief, consciousness comes to a full stop.

I think that this is no less true of scientific than of religious prejudice, of natural than of supernatural belief. So I suggest the possibility that even the scientifically hypothesized "sexual instinct" has in it an element allied to the ready-made "beliefs" of the social mind through which man's feeble intelligence has been unconsciously duped into the pleasant apathy of premature conclusiveness. It is extraordinary how often in the course of man's conscious evolution his thought has been blindly arrested by the subtle captivation of a ready-to-hand formulation.

It is needful that we check our pace just here in respect to the belief that has become crystallized in our consciousness under the conception of the "sexual instinct." It would be interesting to know whether the sexual instinct as we see it everywhere rampant—in frank, in covert, or in symbolic form —*is* the primary, inherent, and "normal" impulse we have learned to regard it. It would be interesting to know whether this conception is fathered by the facts or whether the wish is here father to the observation. It would be interesting to know whether some prejudice or partiality has not entered in and given form to the conception underlying the popular connotation. In a word, it would be interesting to discover whether, in the popular acceptation of the "biology" of the sexual instinct, the social consciousness—therefore our own consciousness—is not itself the victim of an unsuspected complex. Supposing my position to be justified, to ignore the question is nothing else than to shirk the obligations of the very aim for which psychoanalysis stands, that of analyzing, wherever manifest, the vicarious deviations of the unconscious.

The material to which my observations were confined in studying the problem of human consciousness in my psychoanalytic practice was identical with that to which Freud applied himself, namely, those intense reactions of feeling to be seen in that subjective type of individual known as neurotic. The quality in these personalities which more and more forced itself on my recognition was a certain organic fidelity of feeling, a certain insistent unitariness or harmony of reaction in the sphere of feeling-tendencies which appeared to constitute the very law of their being. I do not know how else to express it. Such individuals seem by nature pledged to an organic consonance of personality. Whatever jars on their unitariness or harmony in the affective sphere, whatever clashes with this native integrity or sincerity of consciousness, seems to so outrage the personality as to effect a deadlock throughout the entire system of constructive processes which are the natural determinants of their growth.

In the light of my observation of the neuroses occurring in personalities adequate to the constructive discipline of psychoanalysis, I can no longer interpret these processes as primarily manifestations of disease, but, on the contrary, must regard them as indications of the miscarriage of an inherent health. These conditions seem to me interpretable as disease processes only when related to the arbitrary if currently popular criterion of normality. In the terms of a psychoanalysis that is free and unvitiated by the consensus of popular prejudice, normality can be adequately interpreted only as an expression of the social unconscious. From the standpoint of a social analysis, it would be difficult to conceive of any phase of mental experience less representative of health, growth, and conscious evolution than "normality." Its manifold symptom-reactions are characteristic of the social unconscious and habitually concealed under the familiar mechanism of vicarious compromise and distortion.

Edward Carpenter makes these prescient remarks on the nature of health and disease in both their physical and their mental, or psychic, aspects:

When we come to analyse the conception of Disease, physical or mental, in society or in the individual, it evidently means, as already hinted once or twice, *loss of unity*. Health, therefore, should mean unity, and it is curious that the history of the word entirely corroborates this idea. As is well known, the words health, whole, holy, are from the same stock; and they indicate to us the fact that far back in the past those who created this group of words had a conception of the meaning of Health very different from ours, and which they embodied unconsciously in the word itself and its strange relatives. . . .

According then to the elder conception, and perhaps according to an elder experience, man, to be really healthy, must be a unity, an entirety—his more external and momentary self standing in some kind of filial relation to his more universal and incorruptible part—so that not only the remotest and outermost regions of the body, and all the assimilative, secretive, and other processes belonging thereto, but even the thoughts and passions of the mind itself, stand in direct and clear relationship to it, the final and absolute transparency of the mortal creature.[3]

My altered viewpoint with respect to the problems of psychoanalysis leads me to feel that there is the need to adopt a far larger and more inclusive attitude toward them than that of the originally clinical position of Freud. I think that there is the growing need that we recognize a wholly unrestricted *sociological* outlook, in addition to the clinical aim of psychoanalysis. Such a sociological aim is indispensable to an unbiased conception of the freedom of individual growth. As I see it, the psychoanalytic situation offers a choice between two distinct positions—the one clinical and prescriptive, the other sociological and empirical. Between the two positions there can be no compromise, for, though the clinical and the sociological positions are identical in point of method, they are in principle, as well as in their scope and aim, totally opposed to each other.[4]

I confess that my early position was in the fullest sense clinical, growing as it did out of my own traditions and initiated by the teaching of Freud. With other Freudians, I accepted the interpretation of the neuroses which attributed them to the frustration of a primary, biological urge actuated in the sexual instinct. I accepted the process of cure as one consisting in the patient's recognition, through analysis, of inhibited sexual trends and of his adapting them to the social scheme in a manner consistent with the prevailing social ethic. Accordingly, I accepted the doctrine of the necessity of an adequate sublimation as far as possible. If it were not possible, I accepted its corollary of recourse to such moral control as should safeguard the interests of society until the advent of the beneficent if somewhat precarious day when what seemed the only complete and normal solution of life's vicissitudes should be realized at last in the final consummation of marriage!

I say that formerly I heartily subscribed to this clinical regime in all its tenets. Indeed, I do not hesitate to say even today that, from a clinical point of view, I can conceive of nothing better. But I feel that there is something a good deal better than a clinical point of view when dealing with the problem of the analytically adapted neurotic personality, namely, a sociological point of view or a point of view of social health, of human evolution, of individual growth. From this point of view, the exclusively clinical position of conventional psychoanalysis is untenable. Insofar as it is prescriptive, it is suggestive; insofar as it subscribes to a program, it is not free; insofar as it is biased by a preconception of normality and fails to see that normality is but the common pool of reactions embodied in the social unconscious, it is not psychoanalytic.

A patient's understanding and acceptance of life are possible only in the degree in which the analyst has come in himself to an understanding and acceptance of life. A patient is hampered in his understanding just insofar as the analyst hampers him through his own reluctance to understand. Through the preconceived attitude of our normal, clinical, orthodox fashion of thinking, we necessarily lose sight of the fact that a patient may sometimes sense far more of truth than the physician who undertakes to treat him, that he has within him a far greater capacity for life from the point of view of personality, fidelity, or feeling. It is not realized that a patient may prove to be far less hampered by the conventional and prescriptive than is his medical consultant, that he is certainly far less dominated by that complex of the social unconscious that is specifically *medical* than is the analyst to whom he appeals for the release of his personality.

The feeling of the need for a sociological analysis, as contrasted with the present clinical analysis, has been gradually forced on me with the recognition of the characterological trend I have come to regard as belonging to a preconscious mode of experience that has not yet received the psychological recognition that is its due. The evidence has grown steadily more convincing that this preconscious matrix of personality persists as a sort of background of consciousness, representing a biologically permanent mode that is inherent in human development. Where this trend predominates, we find a native simplicity; an ineradicable longing for the beautiful and harmonious; a steadfast love of truth; a deep sense of sympathy, helpfulness, and human fellowship. The preconscious type of personality is sensitive, inspirational, intuitive, and creative. As I have said, the essential characteristic of this most significant but as yet unrecognized type of human functioning is an innate consonance of feeling.

I think that such a manifestation is to be seen in the really great humanitarians, the men and women who have seen to the core of life, who have sensed the world's need, and who, because of the vision they have been vouchsafed of some deep and significant truth, have stood ready to toss aside at a moment their own lives for the commonweal. I think that this behavior expression has always given indication of its presence in the constitution of the body social. It has been represented by a certain contemplative religious spirit. Through all periods of history, these personalities have occupied a distinct place in the social fabric, tending to unite themselves in circumscribed groups or orders.

It is characteristic of these individuals that they tend to create definite systems of thought and turn to the worship of some fanciful ideal embodied in the concept of a transcendental personality commonly expressed as "God." Of course, in this expression there is the manifest betrayal of the infantile. In the beliefs of these cloistered groups, one sees evidence of the mythical, fanciful, and hallucinatory, pertaining to the sphere of unreality. I suggest, though, that these beliefs are symptomatic of an element that is too intrinsic and too fundamental to the constitution of the social and individual organism to be regarded as negligible or as explicable on the basis of a merely secondary, sublimatory reaction.

The same element is to be seen in the creations of great artists, poets, and novelists, as well as in the lives of religionists. That is, the adjustment of the artist is made on the basis of an assimilation of the mode of consciousness we have seen to be primary and harmonious, with resulting sublimations in internal, subjective activities. Now, the neurotic is the individual who *through repression* fails in his attempt to assimilate in his adaptation this primary, infantile affectivity and in whom, therefore, are frustrated those sublimations which are the expression of the artist. When we consider the essential quality, the underlying motive, of the artist, we find that it consists of sensitivity to beauty, to fitness, to proportion—whether expressed in color, form, or sound. Thus, in its essence, the source of the artist's inspiration is the love of the harmonious. Since the essence of beauty is harmony and since harmony is the aesthetic expression of that which in its moral relation is truth, the essence of what we may call the artist's supersensitivity to beauty is his innate sense of truth.

My thesis is that, since this inherent harmony—which in the artist is sublimated through his creative genius into an expression of beauty—is an inspiration toward truth, the impulse of the artist represents a vitally *moral* trend. In like manner, the impulse of the neurotic—which is but the thwarted, repressed, and introverted manifestation of the same life force—represents, in its essence, a vitally moral impetus.[5]

As the artist's sublimation is inherently moral in that it is nature's successful quest for expression of that harmony which is truth, so the neurotic's defeated sublimation is also intrinsically moral in that it is equally nature's quest for that same organic harmony, albeit frustrated and unsuccessful. The love of beauty and of truth belongs to the unitary, preconscious sphere, and it follows that in this sense the mental life is in its very source moral. It is this that I call the "organic morality of consciousness."[6] In my interpretation, the suffering of the neurotic patient, into whatever disfigured and ill-shapen forms his stifled nature may have been tortured, is the frantic outcry of an inherently moral organism against the outrage of artificial repression and untruth.*

Repression consists of a limitation, a prohibition on the life or love component. We have seen that this component is developmentally an extension of the organic phase of consciousness whose continuity we have traced to those affective satisfactions which the infant experiences in his absorbing union in maternal love.

With the so-called normal—that is, average—individual, the process of receding subjectivity and correspondingly increasing objectivation advances to a seemingly successful issue. But, as we know, the neurotic, in his supersubjectivity, tends to linger with the original model of his infant love. With his gradual adaptation or objectivation of experience, there is the persistence of a preconscious subjectivity whereby he ever seeks to reincarnate his cherished union with the mother.

* In later writings, Burrow's emphasis on the contrast between neurotic and normal dropped away. He came to regard them both as victims of a wider disorder of which the individual neurosis is but a symptom. These mature findings are discussed in the final chapters of this book.—Ed.

Freud revealed that the repression of sexualization through the exaggerated persistence in the unconscious of the mother image is the basic element in the neuroses. But it is my position that this desire for the renewed realization of a perfect union, based on a preconscious model of organic harmony, is an aspiration toward an ideal of unity and truth. Therefore, as we have said, the genetic factor in the causation of neurotic disorders is an organically true, moral factor.

Since this factor of repression bespeaks in essence a morally integrative trend toward greater unity and synthesis of the personality, the inherent moral conflict embodied in the neurosis is biologically an economic and conservative asset of the utmost significance in ethnic evolution.

In my view, then, the repressed neurotic personality represents a biologically conserving and integrating tendency in the development of the race; the neurotic diathesis is an index of a constructive tendency in mental and social evolution.

I hold that there is a still-unanswered aspiration in the adult neurotic personality that is akin to expressions of the social consciousness already mentioned and that this aspiration cannot find its answer on the basis of our present interpretation of the neuroses.* In the personality of certain patients, I think that there is evidence of a predisposition that is identical with the characterological trend I have described. These personalities show an unwillingness to accept sex as an objective quest, as a personal acquisition, as a commodity to be appropriated to the ends of a partial and temporary expediency. Men of the type I speak of are somehow not appealed to by prospects of acquiring possession of a woman's body for the night or, for that matter, for a lifetime, if negotiated on the basis of the machinations of possession and of sexuality. Such personalities demand identification with their object. For them, there is nothing less

---

* For a statement of Burrow's views on the teachings of C. G. Jung and Otto Rank, see *The Biology of Human Conflict* (New York: The Macmillan Company, 1957), pp. 39–40.—ED.

than complete union with the beloved. To such personalities, the acquisition of sex is but a partial and inadequate expression. Sex is not an object in itself, but only an incident in that fuller union beside which such partial and temporary satisfactions are but ancillary or even negligible elements.

Motivated predominantly in their affections by participation in the personality as a whole, these individuals represent such a degree of nondifferentiation on the basis of *sex* per se as to embody a quite neutral psychosexual determination. These subjective, nondifferentiated types of personality represent a tendency toward identification with the social personality as a whole that renders them quite detached from the common conventional sexual contrasts. Love, without regard to the differentiation of sex, is the dominating impulse—sympathy, understanding, identification, the prevailing motive of life. I believe that we have confused the expression of neurotic manifestations, as represented in the inhibitions of such personalities, with the expression of homosexuality.

One of my cases affords, it seems to me, a telling example of this type of determination. It is a case that represents what is conventionally described as the dementia-praecox type of reaction.

In childhood, this patient was subjected to the customary educational program presenting the usual strictures to the expression of the affective, inspirational life. The boy presented a certain docility, a quiet tenderness, in his attitude toward others. He was simple, affectionate, going out to life with a certain warmth and gladness and wholesomeness. He was a spontaneous student of nature (I suppose that all children are natural biologists, if permitted to be), and his enjoyments were of the vigorous, wholesome type. With the gradually increasing inroads of popular adaptation, the boy was less and less at home in his environment. One day he was shamed out of his simpler interests by his more sophisticated brothers and, yielding to the pressure of the conventional, he finally had to submit to the demand for social conformity as expressed by the young people of his day. He pronounced it all sham, and a sense of the sham of things during the following years struck deep into him. When the pressure of outside convention forced him from his preoccupation with the natural interests of the woods and fields and his intimate study of animal and plant life, there was a still-further-increased introversion which was overcompensated for in an exaggeration of the intellectual and athletic activities of college life. After two years, there ensued the final disorganization which led to complete mental breakdown and to institutional internment.

I shall not give a full account of the psychology of this personality. I want merely to cite an instance as it is presented in his delusional state, illustrative of the characterological trend of social nondifferentiation and unity of which I have spoken. In the notes this patient made on his condition subsequent to the period of delusion—notes, by the way, prompted by his desire to convert into some process of social helpfulness the painful experience which fell to his lot as an individual—there is this extract:

> I identified the power I was coming into with that of Shakespeare, as described in *The Tempest,* taking Prospero for Shakespeare. I proposed, instead of dissipating this power in revels of imagination as Shakespeare had done, to use it for a more practical end. I intended to use it to create for the human race a state of perfect happiness, or paradise. I did not censure Shakespeare for having used the divine power by writing his book, but rather considered his work a necessary part of the evolution of mankind. He had expressed life in a book. I considered this book complete and further writing superfluous. All other books were merely variform presentations of fragments of this book. My work was to be another step in evolution. Its object was the attainment of social harmony.
>
> Another idea which was called up by my thoughts about Shakespeare was a vision of what I called "perfect sim-

plicity." In reading about him, I came across a statement to the effect that his father had lived in the country and could neither read nor write. I had read that Shakespeare had twenty thousand words at his immediate command. I was struck by this contrast. I pictured the father passing his life in the country, being one with nature, finding the wisdom of the stars and of the green fields and woods. And to this wisdom taught to the son was added, by an easy process of reading of the grand masters of written thought, the ability of expression in its highest perfection. The easy naturalness of this transition from the illiteracy of nature's wisdom to the greatest intellectual expression was shown in the calm, unlined, untroubled beauty of the master's face. This idea I crystallized in the expression "perfect simplicity."

In the spring before my illness, while I was living at the fraternity house, I felt that I wanted to alter the life of the fraternity so that it would represent a brotherhood in spirit as well as in name. I wanted to see established a relationship of sympathy and confidence. I wished we might share in an intimate interchange of thought.

It is also characteristic of this patient that, in the egocentric delusional states, he identifies himself with God. He feels that he is the specially chosen one of God—the familiar paranoid trend. But this trend also characteristically underlies the social psychosis which flourishes normally under the guise of religion. Thus this inflation that is characteristic of the paranoid psychosis, with its delusion of identification and unity with an all-powerful creator, is by no means an isolated, socially exotic phenomenon. If it is pathological, it reflects a pathology that is common to the race, for such, in substance, is the concept on which all religions rest.

In the word which the Hindus use to express their concept, "God," there is included the concept of mother as well as father. In such expressions is revealed the infantile origin of such concepts. In the "mystery" of the Trinity and in the Holy Family represented in Christian belief there is to be seen the projection of the entire constellation of the primary infantile psyche—the matric, the homogenic, and the autonomic determinations. But, after all, this childish regression expressive of the delusions of the insane and of the reveries of religionists is but a fundamental aspiration toward unity with the vaguely sensed but underlying power of good. It is the Nirvana of the Hindu. It is the Heaven of the Christian. But, for the individual as for the race, its rudiment is the preconscious.

Such is the manifestation of oneness and participation with nature and with the beautiful, such the meaning of identification, such the aspirations of love that consecrates to us a certain quality of childhood and that is to be seen in the noble and enduring characters of history—the artists, saints, poets, seers. In such individuals, love is one with life. Love is cosmic; love is all. In the satisfactions of their libido, there can be nothing less than the identification and oneness represented in a unity of all life.

The psychology of "normality" is the precise opposite, characterized as it is by objectivation, difference, contrast. It is represented in the exclusion or withholding of the inherent personality from the presenting object or occasion. Separateness, withdrawal, rumination constitute the dynamics of the normal adaptation. It looks out on the world with an eye to its own security. It measures opportunities, weighs values, considers advantage. Its aim is personal convenience, egoistic comfort, temporary expediency. Its motive is not disinterested, its aim not direct, its purpose not simple and clear.

In proportion to the encroachments of the secondary and ulterior, there is the increasing need of protection and the piling-up of compensatory securities. In proportion to the lack of directness, oneness, and simplicity, there is the increasing need of diplomatic recourse, of tactical maneuver, and of plausible extenuation. Accordingly, those individuals who are adjusted to normal standards must have recourse to innuendo, to appearance, to semblance. They cannot state; they can only hint. They cannot assert; they can only imply. The expression of the personality is always fragmentary, incomplete. Thus, the entire relationship to reality is metonymous or symbolic. Indeed, the more we consider it, the more we shall see how wholly symbolic is the adaptation demanded by "normality." In this view, we are forced to recognize that the whole fabric of the social consciousness constituting normal adaptation rests on the basis of the partial or symbolic.

In place of education, we accept the distorted symbol of the school. In place of man's innate reverence before the Unknown, we substitute the divisive symbol of church and creed. In place of an inherent social fellowship, we substitute the symbol of forms, customs, and outward amenities. Love is replaced by sexuality; self-possession, by the possession of property. For the wealth of our own spirits, we exchange an anxious greed for money, name, and position. For life, we substitute "making a living." Rather than cultivate the natural beauty of our own persons, we decorate our bodies with the cheap artifacts of external adornment. Rather than the quiet communion of the home, we seek the restless enterprise of a household. In place of a united brotherhood of man, we prefer an armed league of mutually distrustful nations to enforce an implicitly irksome peace. Everywhere the expression we see in the world of so-called actuality is a symbolic expression. Such is the inherent psychology of the social reaction we call normal adaptation. Its essence is substitution, insinuation, displacement. Just so far as consciousness, whether social or individual, deals in symbolic substitution, precisely so far does it deal with evasion and untruth. That is to say, it has to the same extent been recreant to its own inherent law—the law of its own inherent fidelity, its own organic consonance.[7]

It is my view, then, that the vicarious, symbolic expressions constituting the basis of the activities representing the social mind are identical with those activities of consciousness that we observe in the neurotic individual in the form of dream imagery. Moreover, the manifestations of the social mind represented in our so-called normal activities are as truly a symbolic expression of man's unconscious as are the symbolic manifestations observable in the neurotic personality under the guise of the dream.

This, in my interpretation, is the major significance of the dream experience as observed in neurotic patients. Because of the sensitive organization of these individuals, the symbolically recorded conflict between their inherent natures and the stifling repression of personality resultant on man's immature and inexperienced efforts of social adaptation is rendered perceptible and intelligible to them. But, in the unconscious of the body social, the same symbolic substitutions are accepted at their face values and flourish under the guise of institutional forms in the popular symptom reactions constituting the activities of normality. Thus, symbols which are permitted to pass through the coarser meshes of the "normal" consciousness in the form of the manifold compensations and substitutions of everyday living are arrested by the finer reticulations of the more subjective personalities. Hence the rude awakenings that result from the sudden impaction of these vicarious images. Hence the conflict due to the resolute but unconscious effort to arrest the course of these unassimilable dissonances. Just as the symbol or the likeness is the stock in trade—the stamped and accepted currency—of the normal adaptation, so the inherent principle underlying the symbol or the manifest appearance is the fundamental and uncompromising reality of the more subjective personality.

In the absence of an analysis of the preconscious element in human personality, there occurs a situation analogous to that we see in the absence of an analysis of the unconscious, namely, its vicarious expression in symbolic form. There is a flight toward the mystical. Such direct symbolizations are characteristic of certain perfervid hallucinatory states of the clinically ill and of such normal expressions as occur in the exaltations of religious mystics. This recourse is inevitable.

Whatever of organic truth is denied its expression in the realm of reality will *invent* its expression in the realm of fantasy. This process is inherent. It is law. It cannot be circumvented by any alternative issue. To temporize through resort to an analysis of the suggestive, prescriptive type is to utterly misconceive both the individual need and the sociological problem of which the individual is the unconscious spokesman. It is required that we free our interpretations of our tendencies to habituation and convention. The clearest *objective* safeguard against the conventionalization of our scientific observations is to return to our biological sources in search of parallel analogies in the sphere of ontogenetic rudiments. We need to recognize the biological principle embodied in the individual's genesis in the maternal organism. We need to regard this principle psychologically and consider its significance from the point of view of mental life in general.

In the primary mode of the preconscious, I believe that there is offered the prototype of the entire subsequent love life of the organism.* I believe that, in this original mode, is represented the biological substrate, or matrix, of that condition of

---

* Ashley Montagu has recently advanced a somewhat similar viewpoint in *The Meaning of Love* (New York: The Julian Press, 1953), pp. 18–19.

Compare also a recent book by Paul Halmos in which the author refers extensively to Burrow's formulations: *Solitude and Privacy*, "A Study of Social Isolation, Its Causes and Therapy" (New York: Philosophical Library, 1953).

See also Ian Suttie, *The Origins of Love and Hate* (New York: The Julian Press, 1952).

See also Therese Benedek, "The Psychoanalytic Implications of the Primary Unit: Mother–Child." *The American Journal of Orthopsychiatry*, 19 (1949), 642–654.

It is interesting in this regard to note that "the Hebrew term indicating God's love for man and man's love for his neighbor is *rachamim*, the root of which is *rechem*—womb." Erich Fromm, *Man for Himself*, "An Inquiry into the Psychology of Ethics" (New York: Rinehart & Co., 1947), p. 100.—ED.

consciousness which in adult life finds its satisfaction alone in an analogous condition of correspondence, unity, and identification with the personality of another. In my view, the psychopathologist will eventually come to recognize that failure in the realization of this principle is the true account of many inadequacies of the mental life that are today but little understood. I refer to certain characteristic neuroses, but more especially to the psychoses. Only a sociological analysis is competent to resolve the conditions arising from this failure.

By a "sociological analysis," I mean, as I have indicated, a broad, unconventional analysis, an analysis that represents the precise contrary of the clinical analysis, with its aim of restoring the patient to normality or of bringing him under the thralldom of the popular rule of adaptation. What may be the rule of normality may not be at all the rule of subjective individuality. That which may constitute the criterion of normality may not at all constitute the criterion of personality. What may be a successful adaptation on the basis of the objective, compromise, give-and-take program of normality may not be in the least adequate to the needs of the characterological type whose basis is one of unity, identification, and harmony.

It is my position that, having freed himself from the pall of fear and prescriptiveness that overlies the popular mind, the sociological analyst will find evidence that, deep within the heart of man, the sexual impulse is not an acquisitive aim for satisfaction for its own sake. When the removal of the compromise social repressions and subterfuges permits sex to be seen in its native truth, it will be recognized as an elemental and inherent principle of oneness, identification, and mutual self-completion in the beloved personality.

This element that we call "love" is as yet but imperfectly understood in the significance of its influence on human personality. Having been sentimentalized through the ages in the sublimated raptures of poet, philosopher, and priest, it is no wonder that the biological principle underlying this manifestation has inevitably been neglected by the more thoughtful students of love and that it has been abandoned to the cheap imitations of love.

I believe that the student of behavior who is willing to face the obligation of carrying his investigations to their ultimate reach cannot confine the scope of his work to the domain of sexuality, but that he must extend its bounds to the larger sphere of love, for sex is but the part whereof love is the whole. Sex is but the half-truth of which love is the completion.* Wherever love is not honest and free, wherever it is partitioned and repressed, it is sexuality. Under the suzerainty of love, physical union is fearless and unashamed. Love being the ulti-

---

* In this connection, the two following quotations from Georg Grod-deck are significant:

Personal sex cuts right across the fundamental qualities of human na-ture; the very word suggests the violent splitting asunder of humanity into male and female. Sexus is derived from secare, to cut, from which we also get segmentum, a part cut from a circle. It conveys the idea that man and woman once formed a unity, that together they make a complete whole, the perfect circle of the individuum and that both sec-tions share the properties of this individuum. These suggestions are of course in harmony with the ancient Hebrew legend, which told how God first created a human being who was both male and female, Adam-Lilith, and later sawed this asunder. We find a similar idea in the writ-ings of Plato. . . .

In the history of the human individuum the beginning and the end of life, conception and death, may be looked upon as two supreme efforts to achieve unity on the part of separated sections. There is a good deal in life that we find easier to accept and understand if we adopt the view that the individuum, having been violently split into sections, sexus, desires passionately to unite itself afresh. It gives, for instance, an additional explanation of the urge of the two sexes towards each other, while the consuming love between mother and son is seen no longer as the mere result of childish experiences but as an inevitable human destiny: even homo-sexual passion is given some sort of basis.

The World of Man (New York: Funk & Wagnalls; London: Vision Press Ltd., 1951), pp. 128–129, 220.

Compare also William E. Galt, "The Male–Female Dichotomy in Hu-man Behavior: A Phylobiological Evaluation," *Psychiatry*, 6 (1943), 1–14.—ED.

mate completion of two personalities in each other, sex must wait on love. But it has not waited. It has rushed in and taken unwarranted possession, for sexuality is the way of least resistance. It is the short-circuiting of the currents of personality. It gives precedence to the reflex path of the wish, rather than to the complete circuit through the conscious sphere of understanding and personality. This is the meaning of the unconscious, the metonymy of hysteria. It is the part for the whole; it is secrecy and concealment in place of forthrightness and acceptance, fearful self-protectiveness rather than conscious self-realization and growth.

If sexuality or the symbol is paramount in life, then civilization will continue on its present symbolic, conventional basis of adaptation. But, in the conscious scheme of life, there appears to be a characterological type whose subjective inner perception inevitably pierces the gossamer of symbol and substitution, rendering life untenable except under terms of conscious unity and understanding. Thus it behooves the sociologist to take cognizance of the possibility of an order of conscious beings with a new and larger sense of the meaning of life as interpreted in terms of the biological principle of unity man has inarticulately felt but as yet only understood as love.

NOTES

1. The great difficulty under which this concept labors is the circumstance that the social consciousness assumes a basis that is two-dimensional, so that, if one repudiates what is commonly called morality, the social mind immediately reverts to the opposite extension and assumes that one is advocating a program of immorality; if one today disclaims the basis for consensual social behavior, one is at once interpreted as advocating a course of personal misbehavior. If, as in the present instance, I use the term "nonsexual," I am immediately interpreted as employing a

usage that inevitably implies the opposite of what we know as sexual, that is, as implying a condition of enforced abstinence or of an ascetic program induced through an artificial self-repression.

2. Edward Carpenter, *My Days and Dreams* (New York: Charles Scribner's Sons, 1916), pp. 203–204.

3. Edward Carpenter, *Civilisation, Its Cause and Cure* (New York: Charles Scribner's Sons, 1921), pp. 14–17.

4. Trigant Burrow, "The Group Method of Analysis," *The Psychoanalytic Review*, XIV (1927), 268–280.

5. "Moral" is here used in the sense of a striving toward conformity to inherent law, to organic order, and is in no sense to be allied with the morality of convention.

6. Trigant Burrow, "Character and the Neuroses," *The Psychoanalytic Review*, I (1914), 121–128.

7. In speaking of the substitutive type of adaptation, D. H. Lawrence says:

> For what does goodness mean? It means, in the end, being like everybody else, and not having a soul to call your own. Certainly you mustn't have a feeling to call your own. You must be good, and feel exactly what is expected of you, which is just what other people feel. Which means that in the end you feel nothing at all, all your feeling has been killed out of you. And all that is left is the artificial stock emotion which comes out with the morning papers.

"Enslaved by Civilisation," *Assorted Articles* (New York: Alfred A. Knopf, 1930), p. 142.

The Preconscious in
Everyday Life

5

Literature, Music, and
Aspects of Nature

In the preceding chapters, I have outlined my concept of the preconscious, or the "nest instinct," and have suggested its relationship to various behavior expressions. Now I should like to present other phenomena of a more general nature which also can be adequately explained, it seems to me, only in reference to the principle of primary identification. This and succeeding chapters will be devoted to the more commonplace indications of an early mode of awareness that precedes the interaffective, or transference, phase of "normal" or psychoneurotic adaptation. I shall attempt to show that there are moods and symbols specific to this early, undifferentiated, organismic phase of the individual's experience. Perhaps the finer intimations of this basic biological accord are to be found in music, poetry, and the arts generally; but everywhere, throughout all the activities of man, there are evidences, however masked by distorted symbols, of a neglected expression that is organic.

As the reader will recall, the symbols expressive of the pre-conscious mode are by no means sharply demarcated from those of the later divisive, or unconscious, mode. This is to be expected, for there is nowhere in man's present conscious behavior evidence of any clear demarcation between those first physiological activities of the organism expressive of unity and integration and the striving, divisive, or so-called sexual reactions which gradually come to characterize the organism's later behavior. Accordingly, in the field of our outer symptomatology, these two trends—the unitary and the divisive—not infrequently exist side by side in constituting what we experience as our everyday moods; or they may converge to form a single symbolic narrative, whether occurring in legend, dream, charade, or allegory.

I should like first to call attention to certain passages in literature which refer to those commonplace, indescribable moods that characterize the subjective experience of everyday life—the effect produced in us by certain perceptual impressions, such, for example, as come to us when looking out over a limitless stretch of sea, the response to the soft, uncertain glow of twilight, or to moonlight, with its indefinite shadows, particularly moonlight on water, or perhaps when listening to music at dusk:

> Music that gentlier on the spirit lies,
> Than tired eyelids upon tired eyes.[1]

I refer, in brief, to the effect that is characterized by a certain quiet restfulness and self-effacement; by the absence of harsh definition; by the cessation of pain, struggle, or perplexity; and all that is connoted by competitive concern. The quotations that follow are offered, not so much as illustrations of literary achievement as because they tend to evoke in the reader the quiescent mood we are discussing.

. . . By degrees the excitement subsided; for there issued from fields, from waves, from woods, a mild and wholesome virtue which penetrated my being and changed all my transports into melancholy dreams. This blending of the calm suggestions of Nature with the stormy ecstasies of the heart will beget a state of mind which I would fain retain.

. . . Nothing can more faithfully represent this state of the soul than the evening this moment falling. Gray clouds, whose edges are slightly silvered, are spread uniformly over the whole face of the sky. The sun, which vanished a few moments ago, has left behind him light enough to relieve for some time the black shadows, and in a manner to tone the falling darkness. The winds are hushed, tranquil and the ocean sends up, when I go out on the threshold to listen, only a melodious murmur, which breaks on the soul like a beautiful wave on the beach.[2]

When the breath of twilight blows to flame the misty skies,
All its vaporous sapphire, violet glow and silver gleam,
With their magic flood me through the gateway of the eyes;
    I am one with the twilight's dream.

When the trees and skies and fields are one in dusky mood,
Every heart of man is rapt within the mother's breast:
Full of peace and sleep and dreams in the vasty quietude,
    I am one with their hearts at rest.

. . . .

Aye, and deep and deep and deeper let me drink and draw
From the olden fountain more than light or peace or dream,
Such primæval being as o'er fills the heart with awe,
    Growing one with its silent stream.[3]

It is when the moon rises over wide stretches of level sand at the sea's edge, that one can most easily sink away, out of the body of one's prison, into the large magical horizons where the weariness of thought is purged, and the heart is at peace.[4]

Many a writer has identified the earth itself with the totality of feeling of the precognitive realm of experience. For example, Poe writes:

> . . . I love, indeed, to regard the dark valleys, and the grey rocks, and the waters that silently smile, and the forests that sigh in uneasy slumbers, and the proud watchful mountains that look down upon all—I love to regard these as themselves but the colossal members of one vast animate and sentient whole—a whole whose form (that of the sphere) is the most perfect and most inclusive of all. . . .[5]

Then there is the effect produced in consciousness by certain forms of music—the state of feeling, the inexplicable mode of consciousness produced by the experience we designate in objective symbols as, for example, Bach's "Melody on the G String." Consider the greatly heightened effect of music induced by a harmonious setting, for instance, when listening to an organ in an empty, silent church, especially at the close of a day marked by unusual stress or pain, or the sound of church bells echoing at evening across distant meadows.

> The curfew tolls the knell of parting day,
>   The lowing herd winds slowly o'er the lea,
> The plowman homeward plods his weary way,
>   And leaves the world to darkness and to me.[6]

In speaking of music, Thomas Whitney Surette says:

> There is in every one of us a region of sensibility in which mind and emotion are blended and from which the imagination acts, and it is to this sensibility that music appeals.

Then, swept away from staid objective terms by the elemental mood he is attempting to convey, he exclaims:

> . . . As you listen you have lived a thousand lives; dream after dream has dissolved itself in your consciousness; each mo-

ment has been a perfect and complete existence in itself. When it is finished, you awake to what you call happiness or unhappiness, peace or struggle, satisfaction or chagrin; the unreal spectacle of the world imposes itself upon you again; you are once more a human being. . . . You can not understand music by translating it into other terms, or by preserving your association with the world in which you live. Mind and feeling, sublimated by the magic of these sounds, must detach themselves and rise to a world of pure imagination where there is no locality.

. . . We make a far-away heaven to answer this universal cry, when our hand is on the very doorlatch. . . . Where *can* heaven be if not here?[7]

We have already indicated the inadequacy of the cognitive functions—of "knowing," sign, and symbol—to communicate the unified precognitive experience, and we shall discuss this matter more fully in Chapter 7. It is interesting in this connection that Nietzsche speaks of the "absolute sovereignty" of music. He says: "By no means is it possible for language adequately to render the cosmic symbolism of music, for the very reason that music . . . symbolizes a sphere which is above all appearance and before all phenomena."[8]

Occasionally language adds to the grace of form and rhythm the recollection of scenes in which there is this harmonious quality or influence we may recall but cannot name. Consider the following stanza from Browning's "Love among the Ruins":

> Where the quiet-coloured end of evening smiles
>   Miles and miles
> On the solitary pastures where our sheep
>   Half-asleep
> Tinkle homeward thro' the twilight, stray or stop
>   As they crop—

I believe that it is of this quality that Edward Carpenter, himself a poet of very unusual vision, speaks in the following passage:

It is a curious question—and one which literary criticism has never yet tackled—why it is that certain books, or certain passages in books, will bear reading over and over again without becoming stale; that you can return to them after months or years and find entirely new meanings in them which had escaped you on the first occasion; and that this can even go on happening time after time, while other books and passages are exhausted at the first reading and need never be looked at again. How is it possible that the same phrase or concatenation of words should bear within itself meaning behind meaning, horizon after horizon of significance and suggestion? Yet such undoubtedly is the case. Portions of the poetic and religious literature of most countries, and large portions of books like *Leaves of Grass*, the *Bhagavat Gita*, Plato's *Banquet*, Dante's *Divina Commedia*, have this inexhaustible germinative quality. One returns to them again and again, and continually finds fresh interpretations lurking beneath the old and familiar words.

. . . Anyhow the matter is a most mysterious one; but as a fact it remains, and demands explanation.[9]

Carpenter goes on to speak of one of his own books, *Towards Democracy*, as possessing this "central quality and kind of other-dimensional solidity," as contrasted with other writings of his in which there mainly occur mere "views" and "aspects." And he concludes by saying, "my experiences in writing it have corroborated that feeling." There is this same underlying, unfathomable meaning in the most significant and permanent achievement of art, for example in painting and sculpture and in architecture, or, as Ruskin called it, "frozen music."

The mystery of this harmonious mood or feeling that appears to lie behind certain experiences, exerting its potency yet challenging recognition, seems at times very near solution, so vividly does it impress itself on the consciousness of highly intuitive writers. It appears sometimes with them almost to demand conscious analysis. John Cowper Powys—a sensitive, neurotic soul, if ever there was one—speaks of these moods, "those whispers and rumours, those signs and signals, which come and go so magically and wantonly about the path of us all ... these chance hieroglyphics of the Moving Finger should be, according to my imagination of my wayfaring, turning-points and conversions of deep spiritual significance."[10]

There is, then, the sensing of a more unitary, cohesive type of experience which holds deep meaning for man but which has been largely blocked or distorted in "normal" adult consciousness. In this earlier mode of being, differentiation and cognition play little part. The sense of inner completeness and the feeling-continuity with all things is the essence of this mood. There has not yet been the splitting asunder of an organismic response which includes the "thou" as well as the "I" and the endless entail of harsh dichotomies which this primary dissociation engenders.

Tennyson speaks of this mood as

> a kind of waking trance I have frequently had, quite up from boyhood, when I have been all alone. . . . This has generally come upon me through repeating my own name two or three times to myself, silently, till all at once, as it were, out of the intensity of the consciousness of individuality, the individuality itself seemed to fade away into boundless being, and this not a confused state, but the clearest of the clearest, the surest of the surest, utterly beyond words, where death was almost a laughable impossibility, the loss of personality (if so it were) seeming no extinction but the only true life. . . . I am ashamed of my feeble description. Have I not said that the state is beyond words?[11]

In her poem, "The Prisoner," Emily Brontë describes this mode of consciousness and the poignant sense of pain she experiences as she feels it passing from her:

> But first, a hush of peace—a soundless calm descends;
> The struggle of distress and fierce impatience ends.
> Mute music soothes my breast—unutter'd harmony
> That I could never dream, till Earth was lost to me.

Then dawns the Invisible; the Unseen its truth reveals;
My outward sense is gone, my inward essence feels;
Its wings are almost free—its home, its harbour found,
Measuring the gulf, it stoops, and dares the final bound.

O dreadful is the check—intense the agony—
When the ear begins to hear, and the eye begins to see;
When the pulse begins to throb—the brain to think again—
The soul to feel the flesh, and the flesh to feel the chain.[12]

In the experience of us all there is at times a yearning to return to this "age of innocence." It has formed a major theme for
intuitive poets and writers. In his poem, "Out of the Cradle
Endlessly Rocking," Walt Whitman wrote of his sense of
irreparable loss of something—he knows not what—that is at
the eternal heart of life. Listening to the night-long plaint of
the bird bereaved of his mate, he cries:

Never more shall I escape, never more the reverberations,
Never more the cries of unsatisfied love be absent from me.[13]

Significantly, he invokes the sea for an answer, unconsciously
turning back to the watery cradle in which he had once
known a perfect unity, a unity which he senses and from which
he feels himself separated forever.[14]

In *The Innocent Eye*, Herbert Read writes of the simple, unalloyed mode of early childhood and of its later submersion
and distortion through social precept and custom. Referring to
his own life between the ages of ten and fifteen years, he says:

[This] is the least genial period in the life of a boy. He has
lost the innocent eye of childhood and has not yet become an
experiencing nature. It is a callow and confused phase, in
which the mind is unconsciously acquiring its social armor of
habits and inhibitions. It is the stage at which the sensibility
of most children is irretrievably destroyed. The sense of sin
or guilt is imposed on the innocent impulses, and actions lose
their animal playfulness. Relations with other people become

conscious instead of instinctive: the child has to begin to plot its way through a maze of regulated paths. How it can come through this intricate process with an undimmed vision or any trace of its original freshness is still unknown: but at least we are now aware that we are involved in an educational dilemma.[15]

The testimony of the folk-consciousness, as expressed in the words of the world's great religious teachers, bears on the power of this quiet inner mood, on the pristine quality of childhood, and on the unity of mankind. To quote a few of Christ's sayings: "The Kingdom of God is within you." "Except ye become as little children, ye shall not enter the Kingdom of Heaven." "That they all may be one; as thou, Father, art in me and I in thee." And then the line of the Psalmist: "Be still, and know that I am God."

I have spoken of the element of restfulness and consonance in music, how it moves to gentleness, we know not why; how certain music with its subtly indefinite, restful quality is capable of invoking a sense of harmony and integrity of feeling. I have spoken of the ineffable influence of moonlight, and I recall that a certain musician of renown, while enjoying the moonlight during an ocean crossing, remarked to a patient of mine that always, when looking at the moon, he could distinctly hear musical notes, which were somehow interwoven with the moonlight. That music induces an attitude of gentle quiescence, that it is thought to "soften the hearts" of the wayward and rebellious we know from the practical application among prisoners and among the mentally deranged.

Again I believe that the strange, intangible charm of music is traceable to the precognitive, predeterminative period of the preconscious in which life was restricted in its impressions, to the two primary influences of rhythm and of tone, or vibration—of rhythm as exemplified in the walking or rocking of the mother, in the throbbing of maternal and infantile pulsations, of tone as produced by the circulatory and peristaltic vibrations within the mother's body.

Music and rhythm are intuitively linked to prenatal experience in this prescient stanza in Rupert Brooke's poem, "The Fish":

> But there the night is close, and there
> Darkness is cold and strange and bare;
> And the secret deeps are whisperless;
> And rhythm is all deliciousness;
> And joy is in the throbbing tide,
> Whose intricate fingers beat and glide
> In felt bewildering harmonies
> Of trembling touch; and music is
> The exquisite knocking of the blood.
> Space is no more, under the mud;
> His bliss is older than the sun.
> Silent and straight the waters run.
> The lights, the cries, the willows dim,
> And the dark tide are one with him.[16]

It is in the primarily organic qualities of rhythm and in the concomitant unity of tone or phrase that we may most effectively study the physiological implications of music for the human organism. In this connection, it may be of significance that a developed sense of rhythm is universally present among primitive peoples, no matter how backward they may be from the point of view of civilization. The capacity for hearing and producing rhythm appears to represent an organic endowment of mankind.

The harmonious mood invoked by moonlight—with its melting of sharp contours and harsh obtrusive outlines—is likewise not unrelated organically to the nest principle. The Germans who are preeminently musical give to this mood the name *Stimmung*. *Stimmung* means a tune or a tuning, so that it would appear that, even in the folk mind, this mood is unconsciously assimilated with harmony of sound, or music.

Poetry, like music, may be analyzed into two objective elements, that is, sounds of equal measure, or rhythm, and harmony of tone, or rhyme. But much of the music that we call great—the music of Bach, of Mozart, of Beethoven—like great poetry, in attaining its highest beauty and perfection attains in a supreme degree the sense of mystery, a sense almost too subtly subjective to be recognized as such. It involves an element that is indeterminate, intangible, that we may know only as the "unknown"—the element, namely, of mystery.

In the contemplation of vast, limitless space—"great, cool, large, magical, ordered Spaces"—of an endless expanse of sea, of the magnitude of the planetary systems, it is the element of mystery which creates the spell that holds us absorbed in contemplative wonder. It is our sense of the vast beyond, of the unknown, of the limitless void of infinitude. In the uncertain twilight of evening or of early dawn as in the pale, dim wash of moonlight, nature's lines are obscured, objects lose their definition, and the aspect of things grows "mysterious," as we say. And we say so because such is our *feeling*. Such is our subjective state.

But the "mysterious" is merely the realm into which man's consciousness has not yet penetrated. Much of man's thought that is today familiar ground was once desert soil. It is the history of human consciousness that it is ever reclaiming more and more of the vast area of the no-man's land we call the mysterious. Perhaps through investigation we may sink to the unplumbed depths of that "mystery" represented in the unexplored zone of our own virgin consciousness. Perhaps if we keep open the ways of psychoanalysis and do not permit it to destroy itself through the smugness of formulation and finality —that is, through a *conventionalized* philosophy—we shall come to see that it is just through this untrodden territory of the "mysterious" in our own conscious experience that we shall be enabled to complete the circle constituting the synthesis of every truth.

Recognizing as a definite psychological entity this mood reaction which we define as mysterious, what is its biological meaning? What is its source? Shall the answer be that it is sexual? As far as it has been disclosed by Freud, the affective life traces its origin to a sexual source. But it is possible that the affective life, as we have thus far come to know it through psychoanalysis, may not exhaust the affective life as it actually is.

Let us, then, consider this phenomenal sphere which I am attempting to bring to conscious recognition in the present thesis and observe its subjective quality. We have found that the effect of the experiences we have noticed is quieting, peaceful, consoling. The moods they call forth seem to bring a certain balm of tranquillity and self-effacement, to inspire gentleness, to instill in us a sense of wonder and of reverence. There is a note of solemnity, too, accompanying such moods. Further, this state of consciousness is in itself entirely object-less. It seeks nothing; it is without desire, without any aim toward satisfaction. It soothes without propitiating, comforts without gratifying. It is a mood that effaces pain, annuls perplexity.

The sexual mood, on the other hand, is stimulating, exciting, restless, uneasy—whether in its direct aim or in its vicarious expression. Its quest is instigated by desire. Desire is its essential element. Its aim is possession; its purpose, gratification. Thus sex incites to the pursuit of a definite object, and it is fraught with a driving, obsessive quality. There is something wanted, some tension seeking release, and there is restlessness until it is attained. We recognize the sexual urge as "appetite." We call it the sexual "quest," or craving (libido), thereby admitting its urgent, dynamic force.

We have already contrasted the harmonious preconscious with the covetous, unquiet unconscious. In this connection, the derivation of the word "desire" is worth considering. Desire or lust or sexuality, as we have said, presupposes cognition. It is the seeking for oneself, the objective calculation of consciousness, as opposed to the harmonious selflessness of the preconscious. Now, "desire" is from the Latin word *desideratum,* which means "turning from the stars," from the cosmic. This becomes interesting in its positive aspect as well when we recall the kinship of the poet and the lover with the stars and the sky. Moreover, the essence of obsession is *insatiable* desire. The urge of desire may be said to be proportionate to the inaccessibility of its object. There is in the sexual mood the recognition of conflict, the admission that something must be *overcome.*

Through psychoanalysis, we have come to study the sexual instinct biologically and to recognize it as one element in this opposition. But, believing we had reached rock bottom, we have failed to define the equally important genetic factor to which I am attempting to draw attention. This factor must be reckoned with as influencing man's life, determining his behavior, and thus shedding further light on the problem of human consciousness. Our understanding of human behavior and its conflicts will, I believe, be immeasurably assisted when students of behavior take account of this important cohesive principle that is primary and native to the organism itself, being inherent in the nature of consciousness.

NOTES

1. "Choric Song," *The Poetic and Dramatic Works of Alfred Lord Tennyson* (Boston: Houghton, Mifflin and Company, 1899), p. 66.
2. *Journal of Maurice de Guérin,* trans. Edward T. Fisher (New York: Leypoldt & Holt, 1867), pp. 108 f.
3. "AE," "By the Margin of the Great Deep," *The Oxford Book of English Verse* (Oxford: The Clarendon Press, 1918), p. 1048.

Reprinted with permission of A. M. Heath & Company, Ltd., London, and Mr. Diarmiud Russell.

4. John Cowper Powys, *Confessions of Two Brothers* (Rochester, N.Y.: The Manas Press, 1916), p. 156.

5. "The Island of the Fay," *The Works of Edgar Allan Poe* (New York and London: Harper and Brothers, n.d.), II, 238.

6. Thomas Gray, "Elegy Written in a Country Churchyard."

7. *Music and Life* (New York: Houghton, Mifflin, 1917), pp. 182, 188, 190.

8. Friedrich Nietzsche, *The Birth of Tragedy,* trans. William A. Haussmann (Edinburgh: T. N. Foulis, 1910), p. 55.

9. *My Days and Dreams* (New York: Charles Scribner's Sons, 1916), pp. 190 f.

10. *Op. cit.,* p. 122.

11. Quoted by Maurice Nicoll in *Living Time and the Integration of the Life* (London: Vincent Stuart, 1952), p. 64.

   In a patient of mine, a similar experience was regularly brought about by a directing of attention to the self-image—in this case by looking intently at his image in a mirror for a prolonged period.

12. *The Oxford Book of English Verse* (Oxford: The Clarendon Press, 1906), p. 877.

13. *Leaves of Grass* (New York: D. Appleton and Company, 1908), p. 201.

14. Stella Benson—brilliant writer and radiant personality that she was—once told me that, even at a very early age, at about her fourth year, she had a distinct sense or "recollection," of having lived previously the experience she was passing through at the moment (*déjà vu*). Such apparent memories at so tender an age are, in my opinion, to be explained as instances of the organism's momentary reversion to the presymbolic, or preconscious, mode in which the prevailing conscious mode is retrojected, so to speak, into this phase of the organism's primary identification.

   That is, where the organism's feeling-experience regresses, the momentary content of the individual's mental experience regresses along with it, so that one seems in the moment to relive a similar or identical experience "remembered" from long ago.

15. (New York: Henry Holt and Company, 1947), pp. 64 f.

16. *The Collected Poems of Rupert Brooke* (New York: John Lane Co., 1916), p. 58. Copyright 1915 by Dodd, Mead & Company, Inc.; copyright 1943 by Edward Marsh; reprinted by permission of the author's representatives, Sidgwick & Jackson, Ltd., London, and McClelland and Stewart, Ltd., Toronto. Compare also the experiences of Jean-Jacques Rousseau cited in Chapter 2.

6

The Symbolic Significance of Water, Death, and Religious Experience

In the preceding chapters, I have attempted to set forth evidence of the survival of the preconscious mode, albeit in symbolically distorted form, in the experiences and expressions of adult life. The statically, neurologically disposed will insist that it is impossible that the experience of the period we are considering could have any influence on the subsequent mental life of the individual because of the absence at this time of the structural formation in the neural elements requisite to the storing of "memory."

But, in the mental continuity I am affirming, there is no question of memory in the sense in which we speak of the recording of impressions in the higher thought centers, or of recognition, but merely of the persistence of a tendency within the organism. When we say that a glove retains the impression of the hand from which it has been removed, we are not ascribing to the glove the faculty of memory. Similarly, we may observe in the child, during the early months of life, traces of a tendency which doubtless leads back to the prenatal experience.*

It would take us too far afield to enter into a discussion of the many instances in the domain of physiology that are redolent of the organism's preconscious mode. There comes to my mind at the moment the mother's instinctive recourse to rocking her infant to sleep or into a state of repose. She is undoubtedly trying to induce the condition of prenatal quiescence in which the infant was automatically rocked from side to side through the motion of the mother in walking. That is, in regulating the infant's response postnatally, the mother intuitively seizes on an organic association which has already conditioned the infant throughout the nine months of its prenatal life.

Material gathered from literature, dreams, myths, and folk customs affords overwhelming evidence that the significance of water symptomatically or psychologically is connected with the early physiological phase of the infant's preconscious experience as it rested in its amniotic medium within the uterine capsule.

Swinburne exclaims:

> I will go back to the great sweet mother,
>   Mother and lover of men, the sea.
> I will go down to her, I and none other,
>   Close with her, kiss her and mix her with me;

. . . .

* In this connection, it is interesting that a fetal capacity to retain certain impressions is indicated by experiments of David K. Spelt, who was able to establish conditioned responses in a series of subjects during the last two months of intrauterine life; "The Conditioning of the Human Fetus *in utero*," *Journal of Experimental Psychology*, 38 (1948), 338–346.—ED.

> I shall sleep, and move with the moving ships,
>> Change as the winds change, veer in the tide;
> My lips will feast on the foam of thy lips,
>> I shall rise with thy rising, with thee subside. . . .[1]

And there is Walt Whitman's stanza from "In Cabin'd Ships at Sea":

We feel the long pulsation, ebb and flow of endless motion,
The tones of unseen mystery, the vague and vast suggestions
*   of the briny world, the liquid-flowing syllables,*
The perfume, the faint creaking of the cordage,
*   the melancholy rhythm,*
The boundless vista and the horizon far and dim are all here,
And this is ocean's poem.[2]

Melville writes in *Moby-Dick:*

. . . lulled into such an opium-like listlessness of vacant un-conscious reverie is this absent-minded youth by the blend-ing cadence of waves with thoughts, that at last he loses his identity; takes the mystic ocean at his feet for the visible image of that deep, blue, bottomless soul, pervading man-kind and nature; . . . In this enchanted mood, thy spirit ebbs away to whence it came; becomes diffused through time and space; like Cranmer's sprinkled Pantheistic ashes, forming at last a part of every shore the round globe over.

There is no life in thee, now, except that rocking life im-parted by a gently rolling ship; by her, borrowed from the sea; by the sea, from the inscrutable tides of God.[3]

The recurrence of water in the dreams of regressive patients and its assumed beneficence in religious usage and community mores are well known. In certain states of excitement in the insane, the need of the organism seems to be met by maintain-ing about it a constant fluid medium or a continuous bath at body temperature. The satisfaction nervous invalids find in water is evident in the popularity of bathing establishments connected with sanitariums and the elaborate and nicely calculated equipment of these institutions. We remember the frequent recourse to long periods of immersion in water to which Napoleon was wont to resort as a relief from the hysterical paroxysms to which he was subject. The resort to tubbing as a measure to control the convulsions of infants is also interesting in this connection, and, of course, "normal" people find considerable solace and contentment in a visit to the sea.

In the essentially infantile reaction of crying, the face is bathed in tears and disintegrates into the regressive type of features suggestive of the embryonic physiognomy. Coupled with the bending-in of the body and momentarily suspended breathing, this reaction is interesting when we consider its *occasion*, namely, the pain of frustrated ease and the organism's effort to restore its lost modicum of peace and tranquillity through its psychological surrender, its abject appeal for help, its acknowledgment of defeat, and its withdrawal from actuality—the mental concomitants of this expression.

The relationship between tears and the regressive summons associated with the homing instinct or nest principle had often seemed to me to be indicated in connection with the mother-identification as exemplified in dreams of weeping. But the following incident, on which I came quite by chance, is especially illustrative of the relation of the lachrymal reflex to the organic regression pertaining to the preconscious mode. It is from Edward Carpenter's autobiographical notes.

A friend of mine who lived for some years around Lake Nyassa [South Africa] told me that after his return to England he frequently dreamt at night of all that wild region and its primitive animal life. On more than one occasion he dreamed that he was wrecked at sea, and swam desperately to the African coast, if only he might die as it were in the arms of his beloved; or he would make an imaginary pilgrimage from London to the very shores of the Lake, and there in a kind of ecstasy would take the water up in his palms and wash it over his face and head—only to wake up and find his features wet with his own tears.[4]

Tears, the sea, and other symbols of the preconscious are conjoined in Walt Whitman's poem:

Tears! tears! tears!
In the night, in solitude, tears,
On the white shore dripping, dripping, suck'd in by the sand,
Tears, not a star shining, all dark and desolate,
Moist tears from the eyes of a muffled head;
O who is that ghost? that form in the dark, with tears?
What shapeless lump is that, bent, crouch'd there on the sand?
Streaming tears, sobbing tears, throes, choked with wild cries;
O storm, embodied, rising, careering with the swift steps along
      the beach!
O wild and dismal night storm, with wind—O belching and
      desperate!
O shade so sedate and decorous by day, with calm countenance
      and regulated pace,
But away at night as you fly, none looking—O then the un-
      loosen'd ocean,
Of tears! tears! tears![5]

It is noteworthy that in the Bible, the Lord—that is, the primary principle of good—is referred to as "the fountain of living waters" (Jeremiah 17:13). Again and again there is this allusion, and in John (3:5) there occurs this remarkable passage: "Jesus answered, Verily, verily I say unto thee, Except a man be born of water and of the Spirit, he cannot enter into the kingdom of God."*

---

* The fact that the fish has become a symbol for Christ is also perhaps not without its preconscious significance. The Greek word for "fish" is *ichthys*, which is composed of the first letters of the words, *Jesous Christos Theou Huios Soter*, "Jesus Christ, God's Son, Savior." But this derivation of the symbolic amalgamation is, according to Ferm's *Encyclopedia of Religion*, "probably a later explanation, and the origin is to be sought in other connections." The encyclopedia continues by saying that "the fish lives in water, as the Christian lives by his baptism," and points out that "there were many fish gods in antiquity." Vergilius Ferm, ed., *An Encyclopedia of Religion* (New York: Philosophical Library, 1945), p. 281.
—Ed.

There is this concurrence of water and the spirit also in these lines from John (4:14): "But whosoever drinketh of the water that I shall give him shall never thirst; but the water that I shall give him shall be in him a well of water springing up into everlasting life." And from Isaiah (44:3): "For I will pour water upon him that is thirsty, and floods upon the dry ground: I will pour my spirit upon thy seed, and my blessing upon thine offspring." Here is prefigured the symbolic usage perpetuated in the rite of baptism—the restoration of the spirit through water.[6] Under this symbol, the stain of original sin, that is, of divisive, acquisitive sexuality, is washed away and the spirit is cleansed. According to the Roman Catholic Church, a child shall not behold God unless he has been baptized.* Again, we read in Revelations (22:1): "And he showed me a pure river of water of life, clear as crystal, proceeding out of the Throne of God and of the Lamb."

The power of water as a spiritual restorative is proclaimed in many similar uses. For example, as "holy water" it is used as a medium of blessing in the church. This application is interesting biologically where it pertains to miraculous springs. The most celebrated instance is the Grotto of Lourdes, in the south of France. Every year thousands of Catholic and Prot-

---

* Compare this interesting passage from Nandor Fodor:

The Christian religion expresses this truth by claiming that only through the water and the spirit can we reach the Kingdom of Heaven. That is the symbolic meaning of the baptismal ceremonies of the church, and we can dimly discern the presence of the same idea in the age-old claim of mythology that the dead, before they can reach the other side of life, have to pass through the river Lethe, Styx or Acheron. These gloomy journeys, however, are accomplished in the shadow of death and not in the glory of a new sunrise. The pagan world yearned for immortal life as much as the Christian yearns; however, in that age they knew but one instinctual way, through the mother's womb, and the pall of Hades was spread over their anticipations by the desperate nature of the undertaking.

The Search for the Beloved (New York: Hermitage Press, 1949), pp. 231 f.—Ed.

estant pilgrims betake themselves thither, seeking relief from afflictions of every sort. The efficacy of the psychic influence of the water is proved by the undoubted "cures" wrought year after year among "the faithful," and we may note that, according to the legend of Lourdes, it was the *mother of Christ* who bade the young peasant girl dig into the ground.

There are many such miraculous water sources to which a healing power is attributed. The worship of the divinities of streams in pre-Christian times and the feasts set aside for the decoration of wells evidence this same veneration of water sources.[7] A well-known custom, associated with the mystical power of water, centers in the use of the divining rod.[8]

In the light of the preceding data, there seems indicated the possibility of an organic connection between the influence of water on man's behavior and the water-medium occupied by the organism in the early months of its existence. I believe that the further refining of our observations will indicate a similar association between other instinctive behavioral attitudes and the nest instinct.

Here, for example, may be noted the prolonged "holding the breath" that occurs with crying infants, especially when thwarted and angry. The implication here of an organic regression toward the preconscious is interesting in connection with the many instances associated with introverted states, in which there is inhibition of the respiratory reflex in stammering, in asthmatic conditions, and in anxiety attacks. In dreams of "falling"[9] from which we awaken with an *anxious* "start" and an accompanying effort of inspiration, we have an instance of the organic concomitance between the emotion of anxiety and the respiratory reflex. The psychological pertinence of this relation may well be recognized through recourse to an experiment in which one permits oneself actually to fall through space, as for example, in "chuting the chutes." Under such experimental control, one may make on oneself the interesting observation that, through forceful voluntary expiration during the moment of descent, one may entirely inhibit the involuntary reaction of anxiety that is usually present.[10] The relation of the respiratory function to genetic and comparative psychology might well form a detailed study of deep interest in itself.[11]

In this connection, correspondences between early linguistic sources and the content of the anxiety reactions are of striking psychoanalytic interest. The philological parallel in the following instance is especially suggestive. The Sanskrit word *matarishva*, commonly translated "air," is a compound of the words *matari* and *svah*. The word *matari* is the locative case of *matri*, which ordinarily means "mother," but which may be translated as "space" or "the substratum of distance," from the root *ma*, "to measure." The second word of the compound means "the breather" and comes from the root *svah*, "to breathe." Hence, the compound means "he who breathes in space" or "in the mother."

The existence of a word in Sanskrit which embodies the three concepts, "mother," "space," and "breath," offers evidence of deep psychophilological significance, as every psychoanalyst will recognize from his study of the anxiety neuroses and their relation to the mother, to space, and to the function of respiration.* That the word *matarishva* is used to indicate one of the

---

* There are these pertinent comments in an article by Erwin W. Straus:

> In the Biblical words, "And the Lord God formed man of the dust of the ground, and breathed into his nostrils the breath of life; and man became a living soul," breath is conceived of as the principle of life. Breath is the deity's gift to the creature. It "animates" the organism and transforms the shaped matter into a living being. The breath blown into Adam's nostrils becomes the essence of his individual existence. Yet it preserves the character of its origin. Through breath, a loan more than a possession, man and "anima-ls" partake in the divine principle that permeates the Universe. In inhaling and exhaling, the individual, being monadic in its nature, remains, nevertheless, connected as a part with the whole of the world.
>
> The usual Hebrew words for "breath," *Neshimah*, "breathing," *Nasham*, and "soul," *Neshamah*, are in full agreement with the anthro-

primary or elemental "forces" in the mystical teachings connected with the religions of India makes the suggestion here
of still greater historical importance from the psychoanalytic
viewpoint.

As Freud has shown and as the analyses of others have
brought to restatement again and again, the exaggerated fear

---

pology given in Genesis 2:7. The Biblical interpretation of life and
breath has its exact counterpart in other cultures and in other language families. In Sanskrit, *Atman*—which we may spell with a capital
"A"—is the all-pervading divine power, the soul of the cosmos, while
atman signifies breath as the life-giving principle and therefore, also,
as the individual soul. In modern German, *atman* persists almost un-
changed, with *Atem* as the noun and *atmen* as the verb, corresponding
to "breath" and "breathing." . . . In Latin and Greek the analogy with
Hebrew and Sanskrit is clear and striking, as in the Latin pair of
words: *spirare* ("to breathe," the root of "respiration") and *spiritus,*
and the Greek pairs of *psychein* and *psyche, pneuein* and *pneuma,* with
corresponding connotation. The *Sanctus Spiritus* of the Vulgate is in
meaning and phrasing the literal translation of the New Testament
Greek word *Hagion Pneuma.*
. . . Thus, accepting the counsel offered by language, we conclude
that the primary experience of breathing is that of participation and
exchange, of receiving and expelling, of doing and suffering, of acting
and being compelled. In breathing we experience our vital existence in
its dependence and in its uniqueness, in its never ending contact and
exchange with the world.

"The Sigh," *Tijdschrift voor Philosophie,* 14 (1952), 11 f.; *Selected
Papers* (New York: Basic Books, forthcoming).

It is also interesting that the word "anxiety" derives etymologically
from the Latin *angere,* meaning "to choke" or "to cut off respiration."

Anxiety, in French, *angoisse* and in German, *Angst,* of course, may
easily be traced to the Latin, *angustia,* narrowness, which, in its turn,
goes back to the verb, *angere,* to strangle, a word that occurs again and
again as a basic reference in our etymological odyssey. It needs no
acumen to connect with the same verb our word *anguish,* which is an
intense form of anxiety; but even *anger,* which is semantically something in a seemingly different category, stems from the same root. . . .
In Icelandic, *angr* means grief; and in Danish, it is the equivalent of
regret or remorse, something as we shall note, akin to anxiety, so far as
our mental experience goes.

A. A. Roback, *Destiny and Motivation in Language* (Cambridge, Mass.:
Sci-Art Publishers, 1954), pp. 161 f.—Ed.

of death underlying all neurotic manifestations is due to repression of the sexualization of the death fancy. Such is the finding on an analysis of the unconscious. Looking deeper still, however, I think that we shall find here the factor of the preconscious, with its negation of conflict, of desire, of self, and of sexuality; and I think that here, as elsewhere, we shall find that this factor is to be correlated with that primary zone of affectivity that I have called the instinct of the nest.

Consider the recourse to suicide and the refuge from reality that is thus offered by self-inflicted death. The frequency with which the insane jump to death from a window—that is, jump into space, into a void, the precise situation which to the neurotic is of the greatest horror—is, I think, significant from the standpoint of the preconscious.

Let us think of the meaning of adventure, the element of risk to life. It is this courting of death that offers such fascination to man when he wilfully puts himself in the power of unforeseen events. The universal fear of the idea of death is due to the fact that it is ever luring us with its enchanting call; that cessation of strife is what we yearn for above all things. How often one hears the exclamations, "I wish I were dead," "I wish I had never been born," when reality presses its inexorable fate too heavily on us. As Rupert Brooke expresses it:

> O haven without wave or tide!
> Silence, in which all songs have died!
> Holy book, where hearts are still!
> And home at length under the hill!
> O mother quiet, breasts of peace,
> Where love itself would faint and cease!
> O infinite deep I never knew,
> I would come back, come back to you.
>
> . . . .
>
> And a long watch you would keep;
> And I should sleep and I should sleep![12]

In his "Ode to a Nightingale," Keats writes:

> Darkling I listen; and for many a time
>   I have been half in love with easeful Death,
> Call'd him soft names in many a muséd rhyme,
>   To take into the air my quiet breath;
> Now more than ever seems it rich to die,
>   To cease upon the midnight with no pain,
>   While thou art pouring forth thy soul abroad
>   In such an ecstasy![13]

Walt Whitman's carol of death strikes the same note.

Dark mother always gliding near with soft feet,
Have none chanted for thee a chant of fullest welcome?
Then I chant it for thee—I glorify thee above all:
I bring thee a song that when thou must indeed come, come
*   unfalteringly.*

Approach, strong deliveress,
When it is so, when thou hast taken them I joyously sing the
*   dead,*
Lost in the loving floating ocean of thee,
Laved in the flood of thy bliss, O death.

From me to thee glad serenades,
Dances for thee I propose, saluting thee, adornments and
*   feastings for thee,*
And the sights of the open landscape, and the high-spread sky,
*   are fitting,*
And life and the fields, and the huge and thoughtful night.

The night, in silence, under many a star;
The ocean shore, and the husky whispering wave whose voice
*   I know,*
And the soul turning to thee O vast and well-veil'd death,
*And the body, gratefully nestling close to thee.[14] ***

---

* Compare the oldest known suicide poem composed about 2000 B.C. and committed to a strip of papyrus by a man of Egypt, weary of life. "I doubt," writes Egyptologist Arthur Weigall, "whether in the whole

A common recourse in everyday life is going to bed, to sleep, as a wished-for escape. When things go wrong during the day, one says, "I'd like to go to bed and sleep forever." The tendency, often seen in states of depression, to curl up in bed and remain motionless for days should also be considered. The fascination of this regressive state is poetically expressed in the following stanzas by John Clare, written while he was confined in the Northampton County Asylum:

> Into the nothingness of scorn and noise,
>   Into the living sea of waking dream,
> Where there is neither sense of life, nor joys,
>   But the huge shipwreck of my own esteem
> And all that's dear. Even those I loved the best
>   Are strange—nay, they are stranger than the rest.
>
> I long for scenes where man has never trod—
>   For scenes where woman never smiled or wept—

---

world's literature, Death has ever been portrayed in more alluring fashion or so sweetly sung."

Death is before me to-day
Like the recovery of a sick man;
Like going out into the garden after an illness.

Death is before me to-day
Like the fragrance of myrrh;
Like sitting under a ship's sail on a windy day.

Death is before me to-day
Like the scent of lotus flowers;
Like resting on the roadside to drink deep.

Death is before me to-day
Like the course of the overflowing water-channel.
Like the return of a man from a ship of war to his house.

Death is before me to-day
Like the clearing of mist from the sky;
Like a man flowing therein toward that of which he was not aware.

Death is before me to-day
As a man craves to see his home
When he has spent years in captivity.

Quoted in *The American Journal of Psychiatry*, 110 (1953), 315.—Ed.

There to abide with my Creator, God,
    And sleep as I in childhood sweetly slept,
Full of high thoughts, unborn. So let me lie,—
The grass below: above, the vaulted sky.[15]

Homesickness, again, illustrates the call of the nest. The implications of the preconscious also bear significantly on the field of hypnosis,[16] on the pseudoalleviation provided by alcoholism; on claims to telepathic prowess and spirit communication; on states of somnolence, trance, and catalepsy; and on the euphoria of the drug addict. The principle of the preconscious helps us to understand, too, the incidence of religious conversion and retreat and especially the psychological factors in epilepsy and in those psychopathic reactions that mark certain regressive, schizoid types of dissociative behavior.*

But perhaps no outer reflection or social transmutation of this primal mode is more marked than the tendency toward mysticism and the occult conspiciously observable in Oriental peoples. For example, Taoism identifies the individual with all creation, with the harmony of nature, with the "unity underlying plurality." To attain Tao, one must be as an infant, acting not from knowledge but from instinct and intuition. Bless-

---

* In his paper, "The Laboratory Method in Psychoanalysis," *The American Journal of Psychiatry*, 5 (1926), 348 f., Burrow develops this point further. He says: "It is interesting that in its ontogenetic bearing this principle of primary identification has been fully substantiated analytically not only by my own studies of dementia praecox and adjacent disorders but also by studies made by Dr. L. Pierce Clark in the psychology of essential epilepsy and kindred manifestations. Basing his observations on the principle of primary identification, Dr. Clark has also definitely traced to this source the equally organic reactions embodied in the psychoneural regressions of the epileptic." Burrow refers to the following papers by Dr. Clark: "A Psychologic Study of Abraham Lincoln," *The Psychoanalytic Review*, VIII (1921), 1–21; "The Narcism of Alexander the Great," *The Psychoanalytic Review*, X (1923), 56–96; "Some Psychological Data Regarding the Interpretation of Essential Epilepsy," *The Journal of Nervous and Mental Disease*, 61 (1925), 51–59.—Ed.

edness comes when learning is negated and the individual "knows" from within.[17]

In Buddhism, the Buddha-mind is conceived as the void which is "neither holy nor unholy, neither cause nor effect, neither good nor evil, neither form nor characteristic, neither the root nor the attachment of feelings, and neither the Buddha nor sentient beings." In order to attain the Buddha-mind, some Zen masters urge *wu-nien*, or absence of thought, since the mind is not to be in any way attached to or influenced by objects.[18] The state of nirvana has similar properties. In general, it

> means "blown out" as of a lamp, i.e., one having attained en-lightenment through extinguishing all of his desires. The Chinese translate it as "emancipation," "tranquil extinction," "non-production" of the cause of life and death, "non-crea-tion" of the conditions of karma, "bliss," and more generally "extinction and ferrying across," i.e., extinguishing the cause and effect of reincarnation and crossing the sea of sansāra or the cycle of birth and rebirths.[19]

Among the mystical school of Buddhists, the "realm of Matrix Repository" is one of the two great aspects of Buddha. The Matrix Repository has the significance of "to hold and to cover, . . . like keeping a child in the mother's womb. This realm is Buddha's Law-Body of Principle, the realm of ab-solute equality, of the dharmas, of form, of the horizontal cross-section of the universe, of Cause, of Great Compassion, and of sentient beings."[20] And in the Hindu religion the ul-timate stage reached by the Indian mystic (samādhi) is de-scribed as "a superconscious state in which all distinction between subject and object is lost and the One Self is re-alized."[21]

Likewise, the extent to which mysticism and the call of mystery influence the processes of our presumably normal

Western mentality is undoubtedly traceable also to the bio-physical plane of sensation and motivation embodied in the preconscious. Indeed, this element of mysticism underlies and animates many phases of thought and activity commonly regarded as normal. It accounts for, among other things, the self-comforting extravagances we find in the sentiments of the philosopher and the religious teacher. One thinks also of the gratuitous claims to special distinction that people make on the ground of their "mystical experiences." In many reports of these experiences, one finds serious endorsement of the senti-mental distortions which this early unitary mode undergoes in the self-consoling aspirations of adult life.

The religious constellation—with its phenomenon of prayer, its recourse to rhythmic measures of expression, to music and poetry, to song and dance and the arts—is one of the universalities of man's life and, as we have seen, reflects his early, pre-conscious mode or the genetic principle of the nest. Let us consider the phenomenon of prayer and the common and ir-resistible impulse of man to turn to this form of appeal, to the fancied omnipotence of the Great Beyond in the moment of his deepest need, that is, when the stress of reality is most poign-ant. As Carlyle said, "Prayer is and remains always a native and deepest impulse of the soul of man. . . ."[22] William James says, "[T]he reason why we *do* pray . . . is simply that we cannot *help* praying,"[23] and Lincoln wrote, "I have been driven many times upon my knees by the overwhelming conviction that I had nowhere else to go."[24] Such utterances are a witness of the organic element associated with the reaction we know as prayer.

It is not so much that man has recourse to prayer as that prayer takes hold of him at certain crises and, as it were, bends him to its will. I do not doubt that the folding-in of the body which is the characteristic attitude of prayer is biogenetically related to the mental capitulation or the preconscious involu-tion concomitant with the organism's nuclear infolding within the maternal capsule. Is it not the compelling force of the primary affective sphere that explains the extraordinary psychological experiences—the feeling of complete identification, of oneness and continuity—of which we read in the history of religious conversions? Recall the confessions of Tolstoy, of Augustine, and others. Observe how they "feel" the presence of God.

Is not the primary affective mode the dynamic source which explains, too, the enormous vitality of those manifold perversions of the religious impulse observed in the infinite variety of creeds and superstitions in which we see exemplified man's quest for a place of comfort and repose? All the religions of the world embody the element of distortion in that they are in actuality symbolic substitutions for the preconscious mode and not a direct development of total physiological processes from the integral mode of the organism's intrauterine stage to a completely confluent society.

I have spoken of the subtle appeal of the element of mystery, of the unknown. Now it is in man's conception of God that is represented the universal quest whereby he ever seeks to resolve this factor of the unknown. That is, in the concept of God, the unknown becomes for man the ultimate reality, or the philosophical "first cause." And is not the biology of the unknown, or the "first cause," precisely the preconscious? Is not God merely the rationalization whereby is sublimated in man this principle of the nest instinct? In other words, although certain subjective phenomena of experience belonging to the preconscious have been, through popular sophistication, referred to God as the primary reality, is not the truth found to lie in the exact opposite of this statement? Are not these subjective experiences themselves the primary reality whereof "God" and "Heaven" are but the projected symbols?

I believe that, just as we have traced to the secret lusts of the unconscious the mythical principle of evil personified in the "Devil," so we may trace to the serene, self-sufficing mode of the preconscious the mystical personage embodying the principle of "good"—the personage represented in the symbols of many of the ancient as well as of prevailing religions as the one, all-embracing, self-contained, and supreme God.

Through the recognition of the principle of the preconscious we shall arrive at a biological interpretation of those remote, mystical images which have hitherto served man in the dark hour of his unenlightenment. We need to reactivate from our preconscious substrate the essential principle of identification and cohesion (love) that underlies the social activities of man. Naturally, I use the much-abused word "love" in the sense of an understanding participation and oneness with life, that is, the love that is organic and reveals in very truth "the word made flesh."*

As I see it, then, the deeper resistance—the resistance that is fundamental in our lives today, whether existing in neurotic or normal—is a resistance to love as expressed in that cohesive sympathy with which we identify ourselves with others. In the chronic discord and unquiet of life embodied in the neurosis, whether expressed in its individual or in its social form, the essential meaning of the conflict lies in the difficulties of reconciliation between the "knowing," self-interested mode of consciousness, on the one hand, and, on the other, the harmonious and disinterested mode represented in the primary preconscious. Read in the light of this interpretation, the account of the curse laid on our "first parents" symbolizes, as indicated in Chapter 3, nothing other than the genesis in man of moral cognition or the conflict of the unconscious. Accordingly, the Garden of Eden in which they had dwelt in unhallowed "innocence," enjoying in peace and plenty the companionship of God, symbolizes no less the noncognitive, harmonious mode of the preconscious.[25]

---

* Otto Rank's concept of love seems to be similar to that of Burrow when he says:

> . . . Every emotion which is admitted in its totality manifests itself as love, yes, one might also identify love with totality, just as fear, and all negative emotions, are one with partiality.

Will Therapy (New York: Alfred A. Knopf, 1936), p. 197.—Ed.

Thus man has come to substitute sexuality and the self-reflective satisfactions of the unconscious for the larger demands of identification and love pertaining to the primary preconscious. Says Ibsen's hero, "I hate because I cannot love." This is why man invents "God" and unloads on him his unconscious hate by besieging him with selfish, infantile petitions. This is why he evades himself and the harmonious principle within him and hurries from hope to hope, from promise to promise, thinking to find his god in this or that idle refuge from reality. It is his resistance to himself, to his own inherent, selfless, unitary preconscious.

The manifold restlessness and obsessiveness expressive of the ever-driving quest underlying men's activities are but symptoms of the egocentric pride which has caused man to temporarily abandon the inherent principle that is his essential birthright. This can be said whether the reactions are represented in nationalism, commercialism, or feminism; marriage, one's home and children; money, name, or position; literature, art, or God.

Man's task, as I see it, is the development of that common or social basis of consciousness that is the phylogenetic aspect of the identification and continuity we have found to be characteristic of the preconscious mode. I cannot too strongly emphasize that the many evidences we have considered of the principle of the nest do not in themselves represent healthy feeling and behavior. They are regressive substitutions for a total, cohesive, participating type of consciousness and behavior that would naturally be the mature development of such preconscious foundations. An analogy may be seen in the development of the skeletal structure of the child. As we know, the skeleton of the embryo is composed, not of bone, but of cartilage. Nor does the cartilage later become bone. Bone is formed through the activity of the marrow cells, and, as the harder, tougher structure of the bone is laid down, there takes place simultaneously the absorption of the temporary framework of cartilage. In other words, the cartilage is to the bone as the scaffolding is to the house. Likewise, with the development of consciousness in its social, or phylic, form, there is the mature realization of preconscious foundations, and this primary mode of experience is correspondingly absorbed.

In Part III, we shall consider man's mature social consciousness and the impediments to its development which came to light in the course of the phylobiological researches of my associates and myself.

NOTES

1. Algernon Charles Swinburne, "The Triumph of Time."
2. *Leaves of Grass* (New York: D. Appleton & Company, 1908), p. 10.
3. *Romances of Herman Melville* (New York: Tudor Publishing Co., 1931), p. 854.
4. *My Days and Dreams, op. cit.*, p. 231.
5. "Tears," *Leaves of Grass, op. cit.*, p. 204.
6. It is interesting that a sect of Baptists in Virginia make it a condition of eligibility to baptism and to reception into the church that the applicant must first have had a dream in which water has figured.
7. Edward Carpenter says, in *My Days and Dreams, op. cit.*, pp. 295 f.:

    One of the few native institutions of long standing in this locality is the Well-dressing—which takes place in some of the neighboring villages once a year, during the feast-week of the village, and is accompanied with dancing and other festivities. The village fountain or spring is decorated with flowers—sometimes in quite elaborate and ornamental designs—and the festival evidently dates from very early or pre-Christian times when the divinities of the streams and water-sources were recognized and worshipped.

8. In this connection, the symptoms of a patient of mine seemed to me very suggestive from the standpoint of the preconscious. Very early in the analysis, the patient mentioned with much enthusiasm the phenomenon of the divining rod and its infallible

indication when used by him. He was a well-educated man and not otherwise credulous of the so-called occult. I am not concerned here with the belief itself. My interest has to do solely with the bearing of the patient's attitude toward it in the light of his own psychology. One incident was especially revealing in showing the relation subjectively of water to the preconscious. Driving to town from his home in the country, the patient was frequently subject to anxiety attacks, a marked feature of which was a sense of dizziness, so that he would often have to get out of his car and walk up and down to steady himself. It was noted that these attacks would occur characteristically at three special places. On inquiry it was found that at each of these places there was a reservoir near the road, but in only one spot was water visible to a person driving by. Though the patient knew of these other two water sources, they were not presented to his objective consciousness.

Other symptoms in this patient were the fear of being alone, especially in a wide space, and the fear of a closed place or of a situation of detention or isolation; a stuffy, crowded room was quite unendurable and a damp, rainy day greatly increased his symptoms, causing an increase of the sense of withdrawal, confusion, and dizziness. It is especially noteworthy that, in these attacks, there was the feeling that the eyes were drawn in and that they were crossed, a symptom I have observed in three other patients in whom there were correspondences in the other general symptoms. In view of the common analogies, the likely relationship of this symptom to the preconscious condition of the infant, in which the eyes are inverted, is at least suggestive. Most remarkable in this patient was the observation that tones of a certain rate of vibration were also a factor which immediately produced the altered state of consciousness characterized by vagueness, dizziness, and confusion. (Compare Rousseau's experiences described in Chapter II.) His dreams were frequently of levitation, of floating in space, of sinking away—that is, from the contacts of actuality.

9. In my reading of them, these dreams, like dreams of levitation, are classifiable as manifestations of the preconscious.

10. Burrow, *Science and Man's Behavior, op. cit.*, p. 363, n. 12.

11. *Ibid.*, pp. 487–492.

12. "Retrospect," *The Collected Poems of Rupert Brooke* (New York: John Lane Co., 1916), p. 119; reprinted by permission of

Dodd, Mead & Company, Inc., copyright 1915; copyright 1943 by Edward Marsh; reprinted by permission of the author's representatives, Sidgwick & Jackson, Ltd., London, and McClelland and Stewart, Ltd., Toronto.

13. *The Complete Poetical Works of John Keats* (New York: Thomas Y. Crowell & Co., 1895), pp. 293 f.

14. "When Lilacs Last in the Dooryard Bloom'd," *Leaves of Grass* (New York: D. Appleton and Company, 1908), pp. 260 f.

15. "Written in Northampton County Asylum," *The Oxford Book of English Verse* (Oxford: Clarendon Press, 1918), p. 720.

16. I cannot regard hypnotism as anything other than the reinducing in consciousness of the primary, quiescent mode which existed in the original, preconscious phase of the mental life. It seems to me that there is here a basis of investigation of this phenomenon which will place the entire field of hypnotic experimentation in an altered light. Compare Poul Bjerre, *The History and Practice of Psychoanalysis,* trans. Elizabeth N. Barrow (Boston: Richard G. Badger, 1916), pp. 162–178.

17. Arthur Waley, *The Way and Its Power,* "A Study of the Tao Tê Ching and Its Place in Chinese Thought" (New York: Houghton Mifflin Co., 1935), p. 262.

18. Ferm, *op. cit.,* pp. 103–105.

19. *Loc. cit.*

20. *Loc. cit.*

21. *Ibid.,* p. 686.

22. From a letter to George A. Duncan, June 9, 1870, in James Anthony Froude, *Thomas Carlyle,* "A History of the First Forty Years of His Life" (New York: Scribner's, 1897), II, 17.

23. *Principles of Psychology* (New York: Henry Holt & Company, 1890), Vol. I, p. 316.

24. Noah Brooks, "Personal Recollections of Abraham Lincoln," *Harper's Magazine* (July 1865).

25. Our ethnic consciousness bears testimony again to the phylogenetic priority of the preconscious in the legend which records the expulsion of Satan and his angels from the harmony and quiescence of Paradise (see *Paradise Lost*). Satan sinned against God. He would have been greater than God. Thus it was pride which gave origin to the powers of evil and established for man the sphere of eternal punishment.

Our Common Integrity
as a Species

7

The Development
of Language and
Consciousness of Self

Each of us from his earliest years is educated in the use of the names, or symbols, of things. Each object that we see is given its corresponding sound, and we in turn reproduce this sound in designating the object to others. When we consider it, life among civilized societies is lived almost wholly in a medium of symbols. We not only speak, hear, and see in symbols, but we think and dream in symbols. So deeply immersed are we socially in this code usage that it is now quite second nature, automatic and unconscious. The anthropological importance of the symbol as a time- and labor-saving device need hardly be pointed out. It affords man a shorthand means of communication that is an incalculable asset to the individual and the species.

In this chapter, however, we shall consider indications that the undue interpolation of the processes of mentation characterizing man's projective, linguistic function caused a breach in the organism's physiological basis of continuity that seriously impaired its original behavior consistency. I shall try to show how there was artificially set up by this breach a secondary, symbolic authority that stands definitely opposed to the primary authority of the organism as a physiological whole.

To question our established symbolic criteria of interindividual adjustment is a hazardous enterprise. It is to appear as a ruthless aggressor bent on stripping a deserving community of its rightful heritage to social happiness and security. It is to seem cynical toward those most deeply dedicated efforts of man which, despite their maintaining a merely external consistency, have thus far preserved and safeguarded his continuance as a race. But, far from wishing to bring disquiet to either the individual or the community, far from questioning the native sources of human consonance and integrity, my effort is to point, rather, to the existence of a much deeper consistency, a much more basic coordination and fitness. It is to point to a sounder prerogative, a more organic authority, a fuller right, if you will, than is merely symbolized in our private pictures of agreement, security, and self-assurance—a right or prerogative that is innate to the organism of man as a basic and permanent biological principle.

The prototype of this basic coordination is universally experienced by man in the precognitive, prejudicial phase of the mental life that is concomitant with the late prenatal and early natal development of the physiological organism. This preconscious period represents, as we have seen, a mode of completion and fulfillment, of uninterrupted confluence and totality. Within this primary, total physiological process, there arises an unrestricted sensory field that makes of the organism a vast, undifferentiated, biophysical *receptor* as, in the early natal months of its integration, life begins to take on form and definition. This sensory domain finds its concomitant expression in an equally unrestricted, undifferentiated *effector,* or motor field, of still earlier integration, as the organism as a whole more and more fashions its bionomic rapport with the environmental world of outer stimuli.[1]

Though we now know that the generalization that ontogeny repeats phylogeny is not true in all details, there is nonetheless a general similarity of patterns and stages characterizing the two biological levels. An examination of the human fetus during various phases of development cannot fail to impress on one the general evolutionary phases through which life has progressed. Such a recapitulation is equally applicable to the conscious, or mental, life of man as seen in its broad outlines. Many writers have stressed the psychological similarities between the child in civilized societies and primitive man, and we shall have more to say on this subject in Chapter 8.[2] At the moment, I should like merely to refer to the restriction and conflict in consciousness that appear to have occurred concomitantly with the extended use of neurolinguistic processes and the resultant symbolic or pictorial concept and representation of the "self."

In the early life of the race, the impressions that came from the environment were common to all individuals. They were generic impressions or impressions affecting the species throughout. Among these common impressions were sunshine and darkness; the color and stir of day; the stillness of night; skies, clear or clouded; the sun's rising and setting; starlight; the smell of earth; the flow of rivers; the wide expanse of oceans, forests, plains, lakes, and mountains. There were rain and wind, snow and mist, days of calm and of tempest. These phenomena of nature were a part of man's forebears. They did not *think* of them. There had not yet evolved the instrument of thinking that made possible the use of symbol or language. There was not yet full development of the special mechanism within the head of each individual that gave names to these outer manifestations common to generic experience.

The organism was not yet related to its surroundings in any projective, abstract sense. In the beginning, it was only as a unitary whole that primitive man looked out on and reacted to his environment.

Thus, man and his environment were closely interknit, and all impressions were shared by all members of the species. Sensations were also shared—the sensation of warmth and cold; of strength, fleetness, and agility; the reactions to food, sounds, odors, activity, and rest. In his phyletic infancy, as in his larval state individually, man dwelt in a natural continuum with the conditions about him. That is, the whole experience of his common perception of the objects about him was a sensation, a physiological aspect, of man himself. Man's relation to his kind and to his environment constituted for him an undifferentiated *intra*relationship.

In this early season of man's growth, processes of thought had not yet differentiated or set apart any individual or group of individuals. Just as sensations and impressions were experienced uniformly by all men, so were man's interests and motivations—the interest of play and work, of security against the severity of winter; the provision of shelter and warmth; the physiological releases induced periodically by the instinctual drives of mating and reproduction on which the continuity of generations depends. These actions were all genuine physiological responses of an organic nature, arising from man's needs.

With the common awareness of these phenomena, there was also the sense of man's own commonness. The impressions and sensations and the interests they awakened commonly in man ever served the integration and consolidation of man as a whole, as a unitary organism. The compactness of man and environment was continuous with the relationship of the individual and his kind.

In this powerful bond between man and man, this continuity between objective sensations and subjective feelings, between the earth and man's own physiological processes, we may come upon the primary pattern of human awareness and consciousness. Perhaps this primary life pattern, in affording an opportunity for the uninterrupted expression of the individual, offers a clue to the basic meaning of freedom, independence, and equality, for the health and wholeness of man as a species implies the full and complete expression of the single organism.

Implied also were the health and wholeness of future man— of man the thinker. In other words, considering this phase of man's development, we are once again brought back to a principle of unity; we are brought back to the common life of man, to his harmonious functioning as a total organism. We return, as it were, to the condition of the species before the occurrence of impairment to this primarily unitary structure. In the absence of separation or impairment of the part, the whole preserved its function intact.

So much for the vast system of interaction within the animal that is ourselves. But eons ago an unprecedented development took place. A capacity evolved in man that is possessed by no other species. Through the modification of a segment of the forebrain, man was enabled to produce (at first unconsciously and later consciously) symbols or signs in substitution for actual objects or situations. In other words, there developed the faculty of language, through which men not only responded to the same thing with the same symbol, but through which they ultimately came to *know* that they responded in a like manner to the same thing. Through an unprecedented miracle of nature, our organism contrived to take the universe of its surroundings into itself, as it were, to incorporate it in its own neural tissues. A tree or a stream became a vocal sound. It became a spoken or a written word, and a mechanism emerged that related us to our universe of external matter and energy through an entirely new system of receptivity and response. We now became related to the world of external objects and to one another through an entirely different system of neural reactions.

Intensive researches in phylobiology* indicate that man's marked impairment in total relational function today is connected with his misuse of the unique capacity to communicate symbolically. The evolution of the word and the ability to use it marked, of course, a great advance in man's potentialities in all spheres of his behavior. This short-cut method of interchange constituted an enormous economic gain in regulating and expediting communication among the elements of the species. Indeed, throughout the range of evolutionary processes that mark the emergence of man as a species, no step is comparable in importance to his acquisition of the capacity of symbol-formation, or the production of speech. But, as I hope to show, it is the peculiarity of this faculty that it has entailed also a form of motivation which, far from enlarging the possibilities of human coordination, has on the contrary brought about a factor of interference.[3] If, then, we are to understand our behavior today, we must go back, not only to our own individual infancy, but to our infancy as a race or species and reckon objectively with this extraordinary innovation in the subjective behavior of our common social organism.[4]

The acquisition of any new facility in behavior is, as we know, gradual. Much time and patience is required before the new accomplishment or part-function is articulated or integrated into the function of the organism as a whole. As an individual acquires a new part-function, he can with impunity pay less and less attention to this new development because, coincident with the growth of the new process, it is constantly being taken over by the inclusive function of the organism as a whole. It is this inclusion within the organism's total function that is the meaning of an act becoming automatic, facile, "second nature" and of the relinquishing of the individual's specific attention to it.

---

* "Phylobiology" is the term introduced by Burrow to define the group study in human behavior developed by him on the basis of the formulations presented in earlier chapters of this book. The term was first used in *The Biology of Human Conflict* (New York: Macmillan Co., 1937).—ED.

Human speech, or man's use of the sign, symbol or word, is intimately connected, through the organs of articulation and the associated organs of sight and hearing, with man's innermost physiological processes. Though in one sense the word developed out of a social need, its basic origin is physiological. Arising from physiological necessity, the word was as precious to man as an organ of his body. Contrary to Biblical teaching, the word was made of the flesh. It is interesting in this connection that there is among linguists a tendency to develop one language for all people. After all, there is biologically only one people, and the physiological origin of the word is identical throughout man as a species.

The part-function of speech is, of course, a relatively recent acquisition, and there are many indications that the species has not yet achieved the complete integration of this secondary part-function into the primary and sovereign function of the phyloorganism. As we shall see, this gradual process which has culminated in the symbolic interrelation of individuals by means of verbal signs or words appears to have severed the functional sovereignty of the organism of man as a phylic unit. This social part-function has thus been rendered independent of and even antagonistic to the primary behavior principle activating the organism of man as a species.*

There is nothing now among the realities for which man

---

* The following excerpt from Cassirer is interesting in this connection:

No longer can man confront reality immediately; he cannot see it, as it were, face to face. Physical reality seems to recede in proportion as man's symbolic activity advances. Instead of dealing with the things themselves man is in a sense constantly conversing with himself. He has so enveloped himself in linguistic forms, in artistic images, in mythical symbols or religious rites that he cannot see or know anything except by the interposition of this artificial medium. His situation is the same in the theoretical as in the practical sphere. Even here man does not live in a world of hard facts, or according to his immediate needs and desires. He lives rather in the midst of imaginary emotions, in hopes and fears, in illusions and disillusions, in his fantasies and dreams.

An Essay on Man, op. cit. (New York: Doubleday Anchor Books, 1953), p. 43.—ED.

cannot find a suitable substitute in outer, verbal patterns. We are so accustomed to substituting verbal gestures for organic gestures, so habituated to imitating organic needs and functions by means of peripheral organs that fashion our words, that our days are almost altogether given over to verbal imitation. Not only do we talk obsessively, but our social communications are generally on a basis of outer, surface behavior. The very motives of our actions are now placed more and more within the mutable field of outer appearance.

The mood life of man—his feelings and his emotions—is as basic, as vital, and as active as are his words, his symbols, and his intellect. It is, in fact, a predominant factor in the activities of man all the way from the hearth and home to the assembly halls of international peace and treaty conferences. And yet the emphasis is always on the intellect, on knowledge. Man has taken his intellect to the university for centuries, but never his feeling. There have been no courses for the education of feeling, for instruction and training in the emotions. This education of the intellect to the exclusion of the mood of man inevitably entails a distortion of both.

In our emphasis on the part-function represented by the word, sign, or symbol, human behavior has lost touch with "the good earth," with the fundamental medium of actuality. In the physiological transition from action to the symbols of action, the human species, unaware of what was happening, gradually lost touch also with the organic origin of the word and therefore with the organic source of its own behavior. As with so many things he has invented, man has become a victim of his own ingenuity. Inevitably, his word has suffered. As often as not, he uses his words to hide his meaning, to disguise his feeling. Words have even become the medium of differing standards of motivation, of markedly competitive behavior among us. In this detached use or, rather, misuse of words, our purpose as a social organism is not organically coordinated. We are not, as we assume, more united, more articulated, but insidiously more separated from one another as the word is increasingly separated from the organism that uses it. This element of dissembling that has entered into our use of words has thrown man's objectives out of organic alignment, and we are socially at odds with one another. The word that links us now is a poor makeshift for the bond that unites us organically —the bond initially experienced in its individual aspect in the union of infant and maternal organism. In our dependence on the flimsy consistency of the word, we are really at war with one another while we think that there is only covenant and understanding.

When individuals and groups are not in touch with their common environment through their common senses, they have severed the most fundamental, the deepest, biological bond that unites individuals with one another. In the whole realm of phylobiology, there is no more cogent law than that of the biological concinnity between man's harmonious contact with his environment and his harmonious contact with others of his kind. In this reciprocity of function with the earth and with one's fellows, we have a benign circle. The homeostasis that unites us to the one necessarily unites us to the other. This correspondingly common bond between organism and environment and among organisms *inter se* is the fundamental principle of phylobiology.

It would seem, then, that, with the increase of symbol usage, something very radical biologically took place among us as a species. Our feeling-medium of contact with the environment and with one another was transferred to a segment of the organism—the symbolic segment, or forebrain. Shunted into this new medium of relational contact, our motivation, our common principle of operation as a species, underwent a coincident shift. What had been the organism's whole feeling was transformed into the *symbol* of feeling, or affect. It became partitive, mentalized feeling—sentimentality.

I repeat that the sign, symbol, or word has been and will continue to be a great asset in man's communication with man. But, where man's feeling, where his own motivation, where his very identity is transformed into symbol and metaphor, the story becomes quite a different one, for feeling and motivation are not to be so transmuted. Though peripherally such a transformation has taken place, the circumstance entails an organic contradiction in man's feeling and motivation. It has brought about an inadvertent but nevertheless biologically unwarranted overemphasis on both the word and the head that produces the word. And, in this misuse of the word, something has been left out of account that is vital to man's communication with man—a basic element without which man's word lacks the authority necessary to balanced communication.

This lack may be illustrated by considering the neurotic patient whose behavior is outstandingly characterized by an inadequacy of communication. He seems to be out of place, to have lost touch, to be unable any longer to communicate with or to adapt himself to "normal" living. The psychiatrist may "patch him up" to fit into a patched-up community, but there always remains with him a certain indefinable need of something that the community never affords. He may eventually take his "part," as do the millions, in the social drama and thus dramatically, symbolically, lose himself, because in our social dissociation the symbolic part played by each of us is corroborated by those who play their parts *opposite* us. But always, whether he becomes socialized or not, his great difficulty is "playing a part." As may readily be observed, to be a "part" means to be apart; to be "opposite" implies opposition and lack of communication, and in the absence of basic communication there is inevitable disarticulation and confusion.*

---

* In his *Will Therapy,* Otto Rank says:

But at bottom it [neurosis] has nothing to do with sex as such, is only the guilt resulting from individualization, the difference from others and separation from the nearest. . . .

In this sense the neurotic is a "totalist" that is, an individual who can carry out every act of living only totally, while life demands constant capacity for partialization.

(New York: Alfred A. Knopf, 1936), pp. 110, 198.—Ed.

It may be said that, with the development of the symbolic, linguistic capacity, there occurred the organism's—the phylo-organism's—separative, or partitive, reaction. With the increase of symbol usage and the coincident transfer of the organism's total motivation to this linguistic system, man developed a self-reflective type of consciousness. Interest and attention became deflected from the functional relationship of organism and environment and, to a large extent, centered on the *appearance*, or *image*, of the self and its behavior. Man's symbolic function became systematized into the special organization or entity I have called the "I"-persona.* The organism's total identity, its primary interest and feeling, was no longer experienced as a reaction common to the species as a whole. The reaction of the organism no longer sprang from a common center of motivation, of feeling, and of being. As an isolated center, as a unique agent of feeling, each individual's partitive self, or identity, was for him supreme.

In this universal displacement of the organism's bionomic center of gravity, as it were—with the supplanting of the relational function of the phyloorganism as a whole by mere discrete parts or symbolically conditioned "I"-personae—the solidarity of man was rudely displaced. Instead, each "I"-persona was now a separate and autocratic center of motivation.

The individual became a private principality separate from every other, and at the same time the organism of the individual as a whole suffered a loss in the exercise of its primary function in relation to the surrounding environment. Men came to judge one another on the superficial basis of their mental agreement or disagreement. That is, they "liked" or "disliked" one another on grounds of the imaginal advantage of their separate "I"-personae. This bias marked the origin of

* This concept was introduced by Burrow under the term, "the social substantive 'I'" in *The Structure of Insanity* (London: Kegan Paul, 1932). "'I'-persona" appears first in *The Biology of Human Conflict* (New York: Macmillan Co., 1937).—ED.

the symbolic distinction between "good" and "bad." It marked the origin of the superficial dichotomy of "right" and "wrong."[5] In short, it introduced the biologically extraneous element of self-advantage and morality among individuals in place of a principle of relational coordination that rests on the common advantage of the species as a whole. Men did not any longer function in cooperation with their fellows or with their common environment. The solidarity of the species was henceforth submerged in favor of the preeminence of *me*—of the "I"-persona.

The artist who, as we saw in Chapter 4, is closely akin in psychological make-up to the neurotic, has long sensed the isolating, inhibiting, and destructive nature of our accustomed sense of self. Maxim Gorky has this to say in *The Confession:*

> This vile life, unworthy of human reason, began on that day when the first individual tore himself away from the miraculous strength of the people, from the masses, from his mother, and frightened by his isolation and his weakness, pitied himself and grew to be a futile and evil master of petty desires, a mass which called itself "I." It is this same "I" which is the worst enemy of man. In its business of defending itself and asserting itself on this earth, it has uselessly killed the strength of the soul, and its capacity of creating spiritual welfare. . . .
>
> Poor in soul, the [I] is powerless to create. It is deaf, blind and dumb in life, and its goal is only self-defense, peace and comfort. It creates the new and purely human only under compulsion, after innumerable urgings from without and with great difficulty. It not only does not value its brother "I," but hates him and persecutes him. It is hostile because, remembering that it was born from the whole from which it was broken off, the "I" tries to unite the broken pieces and to create anew a great unit. . . .
>
> Isolation is the breaking away from the parental whole. It is a sign of the weakness and the blindness of the soul, for in the whole is immortality and in isolation inevitable slavery and darkness and inconsolable yearning and death.[6]

And there is this passage in *Peer Gynt:*

> We go, full sail, as our very selves.
> Each one shuts himself up in the barrel of self,
> In the self-fermentation he dives to the bottom,—
> With the self-bung he seals it hermetically,
> And seasons the staves in the well of self.
> No one has tears for the other's woes;
> No one has mind for the other's ideas.
> We're our very selves, both in thought and tone,
> Ourselves to the spring-board's uttermost verge,—
> And so, if a Kaiser's to fill the Throne,
> It is clear that you are the very man.[7]

And Sherwood Anderson, speaking of death in one of his letters, writes:

> I have often thought that when it comes, there will be a kind of real comfort in the fact that self will go then. There is some kind of universal thing we will pass into that will in any event give us escape from this disease of the self.[8]

With man's increasing tendency to rely on the outer word, on mere symbols of unity and coordination, he has increasingly substituted make-believe communication for the fellowship that can develop only out of the totality of his own organismic processes. This substitutive aspect of his being has come also to characterize his "knowing," so that, in the midst of his make-believe sociability, he does not know that he is not in touch with his kind. It has to do not only with the word nor only with the organism. It is, as it were, a biological *faux pas,* an inadvertence of function generally throughout the species man, a misuse of the sign or word that resulted correspondingly in an ab-use of his own organism, in a severance of himself from his one and only authoritative source of interindividual balance. Inevitably, in the absence of this native organismic balance and authority, the word becomes "a snare and a delusion."

It is as though, having learned to walk, the individual suddenly lost contact with the internal balance that makes walking possible. Externally, walking seems simple. Like talking, erect walking is one of man's wonderful achievements. But long ago we lost the wonder of it, and now one simply walks. The individual may alter his gait or his posture or even increase the size of his muscles. But he gives the matter no further thought. He does not have to take into account the long months during which, as a child, he laboriously built up the internal physiological balance that constitutes the act of walking. Nevertheless, walking is, as a matter of fact, a marvelously intricate physiological process of balanced tensions and strains internal to the organism. Without man's "knowing" anything about it, these tensions and strains are beautifully centered and precise. Though delicate and sensitive, they are always constant and balanced. They constitute an authority, a basic biophysical authority which lies behind all the physiological movements of the body. Set aside this authority, remove this central balance, and the body drops to the ground.

In the beginning, as we have seen, behind talking, as behind walking, lay the precisely coordinated organism—a delicately adjusted but powerful authority that gave balanced, authoritative meaning to the word in the same way that it gave balance to the body in walking. Yet, though man practically always maintains his balance in walking, he is practically always "falling down" in coordination with his kind through the medium of the word, or language. The word, though primarily and originally backed up by the coordinated organism, may all-too-easily get "out of hand," out of balanced physiological coordination with the body and separated from it—a thing apart.

Obviously, this is not a "psychic disorder," as we call it—something to be treated again with more words. The partial pattern of language is ever clashing with the function of the organism as a whole. No multiplicity of words will touch this impairment in physiological mutuality. Since words are under the dominance of a partial pattern of behavior, they defeat recognition of the organism's primary mutuality, its basic solidarity. The disorder with which man is faced is a disorder that is internal to the whole organism, not merely of the neurotic patient, but also of the physician, of the community, and of man throughout. The imbalance in physiological tensions and strains that lies behind the individual neurosis is the imbalance of man himself. Correspondingly, the problem, the real problem, is not one of individual men, but of man as a race, or species. This problem is not one of external manners; it is a problem in the neuroanatomy of man.

The seemingly almost impossible task of arresting this overwhelming disorder as it now exists among all social beings might seem an idle undertaking in face of the now-concerted opposition of society as a whole against the reinstatement of its primary organic heritage. But the interpolation of the self-image and its attending self-consciousness throughout the processes of man is, after all, an incident that has occurred in a relatively short period of his development. The organic tradition of our biological evolution, on the contrary, is measured in millions of years. One is encouraged to feel that the stronger and more robust impetus lies within this sphere of man's organic constitution, notwithstanding the fact that, superficially, man is obsessively distracted from it.

NOTES

1. The primacy of motor over sensory function in the developing fetus is emphasized in the experimental findings of Coghill and Hooker. G. E. Coghill, *Anatomy and the Problem of Behavior* (Cambridge: Cambridge University Press, 1929); D. Hooker, "Neural Growth and the Development of Behavior," in P. Weiss,

ed., *Genetic Neurology* (Chicago: University of Chicago Press, 1950), pp. 212 f.

2. G. Stanley Hall, one of the great pioneers in the study of child development, adhered to this orientation. *Adolescence* (New York: D. Appleton and Company, 1918), II. 648 f.

   An interesting study of the arresting similarities is presented in Heinz Werner's *Comparative Psychology of Mental Development* (New York: Harper and Brothers, 1940).

3. Trigant Burrow, "Neuropathology and the Internal Environment —A Study of the Neuromuscular Factors in Attention and Their Bearing upon Man's Disorders of Adaptation," *Human Biology*, 7 (1935), 74–94.

4. *Idem.*, "Prescription for Peace: The Biological Basis of Man's Ideological Conflicts," in Pitirim A. Sorokin, ed., *Explorations in Altruistic Love and Behavior* (Boston: The Beacon Press, 1950), Chapter 3, pp. 93–117.

5. Trigant Burrow, "Crime and the Social Reaction of Right and Wrong—A Study in Clinical Sociology," *Journal of Criminal Law and Criminology*, XXIV (1933), 685–699.

6. (New York: Frederick A. Stokes Co., 1916), pp. 231 f., 247 f.

7. Henrik Ibsen, *Peer Gynt* (New York: Charles Scribner's Sons, 1923), Act IV, Scene xiii, p. 183.

8. *Letters of Sherwood Anderson* (Boston: Little Brown and Company, 1953), p. 287.

8

Primitive Behavior, Individual and Generic

In this chapter, we shall consider observations and studies of the childhood of individual and race as they support the thesis of a principle of primary identification originally binding together the organisms of mother and child—a principle which serves as a prototype of the biological bonds uniting the individuals of the species. The general orientation in these fields, based on a considerable amount of evidence, has become much more hospitable to such a conceptual framework than was the climate of psychoanalytic opinion at the time my formulations first began to take shape (1913–1917).

At that time, the prevailing psychological view of the behavior of the infant was closely akin to the theological interpretation that the child is born in sin and must be redeemed by an act of God. That is, the infant was assumed to be primarily libidinous, self-striving, egocentric, hostile, and competitive. He was assumed to be activated by destructive, antisocial tendencies which are brought into line only through a long process of socialization. Such an interpretation is no longer in the ascendancy.*

The total, organismic character of the interrelatedness of the young child to both his physical and social environment is now quite generally recognized. As William Stern has written:

> From the very first day a fundamental fact of life is the passive participation of a common life, and "the other" belongs as much to the child's existence as does his own self.[1]

The relatively late and gradual development of the idea of self is also widely accepted. Kurt Lewin writes:

> [F]or the child, the boundary between the self and the environment is less defined than for the adult. This circumstance is of critical significance to the operation of the environment upon the child. . . . [T]he child, to a greater extent than the adult, is a *dynamic unity*. . . . The child learns only gradually to separate out voluntarily certain parts of its environment, to "concentrate." . . . [T]he "I" or self is only gradually formed, perhaps in the second or third year.[2] †

---

* In a recent article, Ashley Montagu writes:

Searching for the inherent naughtiness and aggressiveness of the infant at birth and thereafter, contemporary investigators have been unsuccessful in finding any evidence of it. . . . Indeed, the creativeness of the organism is directed toward maturation in terms of cooperation. Bender calls it "the inherent capacity or drive for normality." And, as she says, "The emphasis on the inborn or instinctive features of hostility, aggression, death wishes, and the negative emotional experiences represents a one-sided approach which has led our students of child psychology astray."

"Time-Binding and the Concept of Culture," *The Scientific Monthly*, LXXVII (1953), 151 f. Cp. Lauretta Bender, "Genesis of Hostility in Children," *The American Journal of Psychiatry*, 105 (1948), 241–245; William E. Galt, "The Principle of Cooperation in Behavior," *The Quarterly Review of Biology*, 15 (1940), 401–410.—ED.

† This description from Gesell strikes a similar chord:

. . . His sensitivity to cultural impress is so great that his perception of other persons may at times seem to be in advance of the awareness of

Olive Schreiner, that very intuitive and forward-looking writer, gives this subjective description of the development of the sense of one's own identity:

---

his private self. He is aware of the incoming and outgoing hand of his mother before he becomes acquainted with the movements of his own hand. He probably hears his mother's voice before he identifies his own spontaneous vocalizations as his very own.

Arnold Gesell, *Infant Development,* "The Embryology of Early Human Behavior" (New York: Harper and Brothers, 1952), p. 60.

The following quotations from Georg Groddeck are pertinent here:

. . . With the stupidity which grows with our growth we so accustom ourselves to the feeling of self-importance . . . that we forget all about the time when we naïvely held the opposite position and spoke of ourselves in the third person—"Pat is hungry. Chocolate!" What grown-up could emulate this objectivity? I do not mean to imply that the child's idea of the I, of his own individuality, only arises when he learns to use the pronoun "I," but this much is certain, that the consciousness of the "I," the manner in which we grown-ups make use of the idea "I," is not inborn but only gradually grows within man's mind, that it is something he has to learn.

For a long time I have sought for any European word for child which should contain a reference to what I look upon as one of the most striking facts about childhood, that for some time after learning to speak the young child neither uses the word "I" nor seems to have any corresponding idea. . . . The child is indeed the maker of his world; he creates light and sound, tree and hill, house and man; everything is his work. What he does not create for himself out of his own experience is good and evil, right and wrong, conscious striving, self-plaguing.

The World of Man (New York: Funk and Wagnalls, 1951), pp. 82 f., 210 f.

Even Freud refers to "a feeling of something limitless, unbounded, something 'oceanic' and believed that this confluent feeling is an attribute of the immature individual which gives way later to a narrower and more sharply outlined ego-feeling." He writes:

The ego-feeling we are aware of now is thus only a shrunken vestige of a far more extensive feeling—a feeling which embraced the universe and expressed an inseparable connection of the ego with the external world.

Civilization and its Discontents (London: Hogarth Press, 1951), pp. 8, 13.—ED.

One day we sit there and look at the blue sky, and down at our fat little knees; and suddenly it strikes us, Who are we? This *I*, what is it? We try to look in upon ourself, and ourself beats back upon ourself. Then we get up in great fear, and run home as hard as we can. We can't tell any one what frightened us. We never quite lose that feeling of *self* again.[3]

Countless observations as well as detailed experimental studies have pointed up the native presence in the child of unified, socially cohesive, and cooperative behavior trends. Lois Barclay Murphy, for example, summarizes one of her investigations as follows:

The results of this study of sympathetic behavior suggest that it is not true that the child under four is an overwhelmingly self-centered person. He is dependent on, identified with, suggestible to, and responsive to, other people in ways which give bases for highly socialized responses.[4] *

This view is in marked contrast to the earlier emphasis on egocentricity, self-striving, and competition. However, in view of the emphasis on individualism and competition in our contemporary Western culture, it is not surprising that gentle,[5] cooperative trends in the behavior of children were long overlooked. There is the further circumstance that the empathic, socially cohesive response is given scant nourishment in our culture. To quote again from Lois Barclay Murphy:

* Some references to other students who have recently emphasized this fact are: Ashley Montagu, *On Being Human* (New York: Henry Schuman, 1950); Ian Suttie, *The Origins of Love and Hate* (New York: The Julian Press, 1952); J. H. Woodger, *Biology and Language* (Cambridge: Cambridge University Press, 1952); Muzafer and Carolyn W. Sherif, *Groups in Harmony and Tension* (New York: Harper and Brothers, 1953); C. Bühler, "Spontaneous Reactions of Children in the First Two Years," *Proceedings and Papers of the 9th International Congress of Psychology* (Princeton: Psychological Review Co., 1930); pp. 99 f.; M. J. Muste and D. F. Sharpe, "Some Influential Factors in the Determination of Aggressive Behavior in Preschool Children," *Child Development*, 18 (1947), 11–28.—Ed.

Apparently, in our culture, the chances are ten to one that a child who appears to show a constitutional gentleness will get over it, unless a combination of repressive forces in his environment acts with unusual consistency. This is not because there is no such thing as a constitutionally gentle child, but because aggressive and competitive patterns are so deeply rooted in our culture, and so universally experienced by the children.[6] *

In this connection, we may note that the relationship between the development of language, of the sense of self, and of competitive behavior has been remarked by several investigators. Gesell says: "At two years of age the child calls himself by his own name, and shows a new sense of possessiveness."[7]

René Maublanc's observations of girl twins led him to the view that there is a spontaneous tendency on the part of very young children to consider all objects around them as common goods. In our culture, this tendency is replaced by the idea of individual ownership and responsibility which is acquired with and through language. This view is built up by the definitions of the parents, who impose it because it is to their own interest to do so.[8]

In his study of the psychological evolution of the child, Henri Wallon notes that a concept of ownership develops at the time when selfhood manifests itself, about the age of three years.[9]

Just as we may study early childhood for leads in determining fundamental characteristics in behavior, so data from the life and habits of primitive man shed light on fundamental human characteristics that may be obscured in the specialized civilizations of our modern times.

It has been fairly well established that, among primitive peoples as among young children, there is not the sharp differ-

---

* In connection with this point, experimental studies show that competitiveness with other children seldom occurs among two-to-three-and-a-half-year-old children and is commonly found among five-to-six-and-a-half-year-olds. (Unpublished studies from the University of Oklahoma referred to by Sherif and Sherif, *op. cit.*).—ED.

entiation between oneself and other people; there is not the construction of a delimited, individualized personality.* Karsten remarks:

> [T]he conception of individual personality and consequently of individual responsibility does not exist among the primitive Indians in the same sense as among civilized peoples. The individual forms an inseparable part of the whole, namely, of the family or tribe to which he belongs. Especially the members of the same family are regarded as, so to speak, organically coherent with each other, so that one part stands for all and all for one.[10]

Just as young children, when they speak of themselves, do not use the first person, so in primitive languages the "possibilities of expression in the first person are comparatively undeveloped."[11] Further, where a word corresponding to our word "I" occurs in a primitive language, it often has the extended meaning of "we." For instance, the Maori, when speaking in the first person, does not necessarily speak of himself, but of his group or tribe.[12] Willoughby, in his study of the Bantu, emphasizes the same point—the complete lack of distinction between individual and community.[13] †

* L. Van der Horst says:

... It is quite evident that the child lives from the start connected with living beings in what is called a "we-relation." Only later in life, does an "I and you" connection develop. The primitive man and the child have not yet become conscious of their own egos. They are closer to the community of "we" than the adult.

"The Social-Psychological Background of the Present World Crisis," *The Psychoanalytic Review*, XXXVII (1950), 8.—Ed.

† Today, psychology and psychiatry are becoming increasingly interested in the problem of the organization of the self and the boundaries between the self and its world. It is beginning to be recognized generally that this is a vital problem for the behavioral sciences. Cross-cultural studies of primitive peoples as well as comparative studies of peoples have led to the inescapable conclusion that self-organization and boundaries may vary markedly, that the isolated, rigidly delimited sense of self

Students of primitive mentality have also drawn attention to the fact that, as with the child, there is no definite line of demarcation between subject and object. A *continuity with,*

characteristic of Western culture is by no means a universal characteristic of man.

More recent students of cultural anthropology have amply corroborated these earlier interpretations. Dorothy Lee, Edmund Carpenter, Abram Kardiner, F. E. Williams, and Laura Thompson are among the students of primitive peoples who emphasize the inclusive, organismic quality of their sense of self.

In describing the Wintu Indians of Northern California, Lee says:

Wintu philosophy in general has no law of contradiction. . . . Even the equivalents of *either* and *or* are emphatics, pre-supposing inclusiveness or increase. The concept of the self forms one of these non-exclusive categories. When speaking about Wintu culture, we cannot speak of the self *and* society, but rather of the self *in* society.

In our own culture, we are clear as to the boundaries of the self. In our commonly held unreflective view, the self is a distinct unit, something we can name and define. We know what is the self and what is not the self; and the distinction between the two is always the same. With the Wintu, the self has no strict bounds, is not named and is not, I believe, recognized as an entity.

"Notes on the Conception of the Self among the Wintu Indians," *The Journal of Abnormal and Social Psychology*, 45 (1950), 538–543.

In speaking of the view of the self held by the Aivilik, Carpenter remarks that it differs markedly from ours and varies in different situations. "At times it is open at the back, as it were, and overflows into spheres external to the body both in time and space. . . ." "External Life and Self-Definition among the Aivilik Eskimos," *The American Journal of Psychiatry*, 110 (1954), 840–843.

Thompson says of the Hopi Indians:

All phenomena of value in the Hopi world are traditionally believed to work together in a complex, inter-dependent relationship, for the common good, and no one class is dominant or subordinate to others. The concepts of "rugged individualism" and "exploitation" are completely absent, for no individual functions for himself alone, but only as a member of a group that is a responsible part of the complex, reciprocally balanced whole.

"Science and the Study of Mankind," *Science*, III (1950), 560. Cp. also Abram Kardiner *et al.*, *The Psychological Frontiers of Society* (New York: Columbia University Press, 1945); F. E. Williams, "Group Sentiment and Primitive Justice," *American Anthropologist*, 43 (1941), 523–539.—Ed.

rather than a *looking at*, characterizes the behavior of primitive man. Storch says:

> To understand a thing or to communicate his understanding of it the primitive "lives himself into the thing" in a motor sense. It has been rightly said that originally religions were neither understood nor felt, but danced.

He tells us that Lévy-Bruhl endeavored to explain this sort of immediate psychic and bodily entering of the self in the perception of things as a "participation" of the ego in the objects. He calls attention to the fact that, in primitives, comprehending and recognizing have characters entirely different from these processes in ourselves.* The primitive, he says, "does not really have an idea in our sense of the word; he not only calls the object up before his mind, but he . . . 'participates' in it."[14]

We saw that several investigators have noted that, in the ontogenetic development of the child, the acquisition of a de-

---

* Heinz Werner holds that the most fundamental characteristic of primitive mentality is "syncretism," in contrast to the "discrete" character of advanced mentality. By "syncretism," he means the lack of differentiation of "several mental functions or phenomena which would appear as distinct from each other in a mature state of consciousness." *Comparative Psychology of Mental Development* (Chicago: Follett Publishing Company, 1948), p. 53.

Dorothy Lee emphasizes the fact that the Trobrianders (a primitive people inhabiting the archipelago between New Guinea and the Solomon Islands)

> [A]re concerned with being, and being alone. . . . An object or event is grasped and evaluated in terms of itself alone. . . . Being is appreciated as a whole, not in terms of attributes. This is something very difficult for members of our culture to achieve; we rarely value sheer being in itself. . . . Even mothers are often incapable of valuing their children in this way, demanding instead attributes and achievements before they will respond with love. . . . It follows that the Trobriander performs acts because of the activity itself, not for its effects; that he values objects because they are good, not good for; in fact objects and activities that are good for, are of no value to him.

"Being and Value in a Primitive Culture," *The Journal of Philosophy*, XLVI (1949), 401–415.—Ed.

limited, discrete sense of self was accompanied by a growing sense of personal ownership. Students of primitive man have remarked on the parallel nature of these two behavioral characteristics in the transition from primitive to civilized peoples. Thus, in primitive societies, according to Lévy-Bruhl, property tends to be associated with the group, rather than with the individual.[15]

Referring to such authorities as Thurnwald, Malinowski, Lowie, and others, Karl Polanyi says: "The outstanding discovery of recent historical and anthropological research is that [primitive] man's economy, as a rule, is submerged in his social relationships."[16] In seeking satisfaction for his basic needs for food, clothes, and shelter, primitive man does not act individually, but as an organismic part of the community in which he lives.

Just as the modern conception of the child no longer tends to view him as basically antisocial, anthropological evidence supports the concept that aboriginal man was not primarily antisocial either. Many primitive peoples seem to exhibit a marked degree of integration and cohesiveness in their relationships with the objective and social environment.

Melville writes in *Typee:*

> It may reasonably be enquired, how were these people governed? How were their passions controlled in their everyday transactions? It must have been by an inherent principle of honesty and charity towards each other. They seemed to be governed by that sort of tacit common-sense law, which, say what they will of the inborn lawlessness of the human race, has its precepts graven on every breast. The grand principles of virtue and honour, however they may be distorted by arbitrary codes, are the same all the world over. . . . It is to this indwelling, this universally diffused perception of what is *just* and *noble,* that the integrity of the Marquesans in their intercourse with each other is to be attributed. In the darkest nights they slept securely, with all their worldly wealth around them, in houses the doors of which were never fastened.[17]

Although less emphasis is placed among primitive people on the individualized self—with its personalized wants, "rights," "property," and moral responsibilities as the core of social behavior—there is no absence of order or respect for the individual person.* It would appear that primitive man exemplifies the truth of the wisdom expressed by an ancient Chinese when he said: "Only he who makes no distinction between himself and other things and follows the great evolution can really be independent and always free."

My thesis is that this tribal or social coordination existing physiologically among the elements of the species is intrinsic to man. Furthermore it may be regarded as the phylogenetic aspect of the preconscious behavioral continuity existing ontogenetically in mother and child in the uterine and early postnatal life. The following excerpts from a book by W. H. R. Rivers (though his interpretation in no way bears on the present study) may also be considered as an example of the type of human behavior that reflects the preconscious mode of mentation. Though the observation is one regarding a "lowly people," perhaps it is their very lowliness that permits the emergence of a type of communication among them that may be described as intraorganic.

Those who have lived among savage or barbarous peoples in several parts of the world have related how they have attended native councils where matters in which they were interested were being discussed. When after a time the English observer has found that the people were discussing some wholly different topic, and has inquired when they were go-

* Radin lists the three positive features exemplified by aboriginal society as: ". . . the respect for the individual, irrespective of age or sex; the amazing degree of social and political integration achieved by them; and the existence there of a concept of personal security which transcends all governmental forms and all tribal and group interests and conflict." In none of the aboriginal cultures "did those basic and economic distortions and crises arise that had existed in all the major civilizations since 3000 B.C." Paul Radin, *The World of Primitive Man* (New York: Henry Schuman, 1953), pp. 11–13.—ED.

ing to decide the question in which he was interested, he has been told that it had already been decided apparently without word or argument and that they had passed to other business. . . .

Whenever we were going ashore five of the crew would row us in the whale-boat, four rowing and the fifth taking the steer-oar. As soon as we announced our intention to go ashore, five of the crew would at once separate from the rest and man the boat; one would go to the steer-oar and the others to the four thwarts. Never once was there any sign of disagreement or doubt which of the ship's company should man the boat, nor was there ever any hesitation who should take the steer-oar, though, at any rate according to our ideas, the coxswain had a far easier and more interesting task than the rest. It is possible that there was some understanding by which the members of the crew arranged who should undertake the different kinds of work, but we could discover no evidence whatever of any such arrangement. The harmony seems to have been due to such delicacy of social adjustment that the intention of five of the members of the crew to man the boat and of one to take the steer-oar was at once intuited by the rest.[18]

And in *Typee* Melville writes:

There was one admirable trait in the general character of the Typees which, more than anything else, secured my admiration: it was the unanimity of feeling they displayed on every occasion. With them there hardly appeared to be any difference of opinion upon any subject whatever. They all thought and acted alike. I do not conceive that they could support a debating society for a single night: there would be nothing to dispute about; and were they to call a convention to take into consideration the state of the tribe, its session would be a remarkably short one. They showed this spirit of unanimity in every action of life: everything was done in concert and good fellowship.[19]

As I have said, whatever importance may attach secondarily or symptomatically to the striving, the conflict factors, associated, for example, with the Oedipus complex, there is throughout the entire scope of biology evidence also of this primary constellation, this more native, more powerful instinct of the nest. In zoology, there is the odyssey of the eel, as of certain species of salmon, that illustrates this instinctive trend.[20] Certainly no secondary conflict—no Oedipus complex—could account for the organic urge which drives the sockeye salmon, for example, to such epic measures to regain the native waters in which their organisms were spawned. No psychic "conflict" here—only the slow, sure, rhythmic sequence of primary biological processes.

Certain writers have pointed to the common tendency among schizophrenics, mystics, and primitive people to perceive in wholes and to feel themselves identified with objects and other persons in a way that is sharply differentiated from the mental attitude that customarily characterizes the use of verbal images or words. Storch has cited cases of schizophrenia that abound in instances of a return, although in a distorted form, to this earlier, more confluent level of adjustment.

> [W]e often found ourselves confronted by experiences in which the discrimination between the consciousness of self and the consciousness of the object was entirely suspended, the ego being no longer separated from the non-ego; the subject no longer distinct from the object; the self and the world were fused in an inseparable total complex.

In speaking of one of his cases, Storch says:

> [T]his case is first of all remarkable for the example it furnishes of participation. The participation here rises to the point of a feeling of union with the highest. For this patient, in a more definite way than in the examples previously given, the difference between the I and the thou is extinguished. Lévy-Bruhl is right in calling a union of this sort in primitives a "mystic participation"; for without doubt this feeling of becoming one with deity is the central experience of all specifically religious mysticism. . . . It comes to expression in the "tat tvam asi" (that art thou) of the Indians as well as in Mechtild's verses: "I am in thee and thou art in me!"[21]

Here, again, we may call attention to the preconscious mode as exemplified by Christ. His words are replete with intimations of this mode of primary identification. "He that abideth in me and I in him, the same bringeth forth much fruit" (John 15:5).[22]

The trend observable in schizophrenia has been invariably referred to as a flight from or an aversion to reality, as though the sole significance of reality lay in the personality's acceptance of it on a symbolic basis of adaptation. But there are undoubtedly elements belonging to the preconscious mode that enter into the organism's adaptation to the objective environment or to reality. In children, in primitive people, and in schizophrenics, a tendency toward distortion and regression is undoubtedly present when they hold to this mode in opposition to a symbolic form of adaptation. But the more cohesive behavioral response characteristic of the preconscious mode is not to be disregarded as a contributing factor in the organism's adaptation to the *real* world about it.

In connection with this emphasis on the racial or generic significance of a primary, physiological basis of consciousness, I should like to present a dream which indicates how the preconscious, or premental, state of "awareness" may be carried over into adult life. Within the scope of symptomatology, the investigator is, of course, limited to the subjective intimations of a mode of consciousness that is genetically unified, total, and physiological.

Those who have read the poetic and highly intuitive descriptions of the inhabitants of the Aran Islands by J. M. Synge will recall the dream the author had while living with this rugged people of "divine simplicity."

Last night, after walking in a dream among buildings with strangely intense light on them, I heard a faint rhythm of music beginning far away on some stringed instrument.

It came closer to me, gradually increasing in quickness and volume with an irresistibly definite progression. When it was quite near the sound began to move in my nerves and blood, and to urge me to dance with them.

I knew that if I yielded I would be carried away to some moment of terrible agony, so I struggled to remain quiet, holding my knees together with my hands.

The music increased continually, sounding like the strings of harps, tuned to a forgotten scale, and having a resonance as searching as the strings of the 'cello.

Then the luring excitement became more powerful than my will, and my limbs moved in spite of me.

In a moment I was swept away in a whirlwind of notes. My breath and my thoughts and every impulse of my body, became a form of the dance, till I could not distinguish between the instruments and the rhythm and my own person or consciousness.

For a while it seemed an excitement that was filled with joy, then it grew into an ecstasy where all existence was lost in a vortex of movement. I could not think there had ever been a life beyond the whirling of the dance.

Then with a shock the ecstasy turned to an agony and rage. I struggled to free myself, but seemed only to increase the passion of the steps I moved to. When I shrieked I could only echo the notes of the rhythm.

At last with a moment of uncontrollable frenzy I broke back to consciousness and awoke.

I dragged myself trembling to the window of the cottage and looked out. The moon was glittering across the bay, and there was no sound anywhere on the island.[23]

As in those presented earlier, this dream embodies, not only the unitary element of the preconscious, but also the element of struggle. There is the "strangely intense light" which I have frequently found recorded in dreams in which there occur the symbolic intimations of the organism's primordial behavior quality, whether of poet or peasant; there is the rhythm of music, beginning far away, coming closer, "more powerful than my will," "till I could not distinguish between the instruments and the rhythm and my own person or consciousness." But, obviously, there is also conflict; there is the necessity to break "back to consciousness," to the "will." Though there was on waking only the moon over the bay and "no sound any- where," there still remained a conflict deep within the dream- er's "trembling" organism.

Dealing as we are with the symptomatology of unity in its relation to conflict, perhaps we may take our cue as to the meaning of Synge's dream from a passage in Edward J. O'Brien's introduction to Synge's book:

> Picture this later Heine settling down in those wild and desolate islands, adapting himself to simpler and ruder con- ditions of life, taking the people as he found them, and yet somehow, despite the wandering spirit that possessed him, succeeding tolerably well in domesticating himself, so that we find him rocking the baby's cradle or joining eagerly and naturally in the story-telling circles of an evening by the flickering firelight.[24]

With this suggestion of Synge's capacity for deep sympathy with the native consonance of this water-people, we may turn to the poet's own words:

> . . . It seemed like a dream that I should be sitting here among these men and women listening to this rude and beautiful poetry that is filled with the oldest passions of the world. . . .
>
> [But] in some ways these men and women seem strangely far away from me. They have the same emotions that I have, and . . . yet I cannot talk to them when there is much to say. . . .
>
> . . . On some days I feel this island as a perfect home and resting place; on other days I feel that I am a waif among the people. I can feel more with them than they can feel with me, and while I wander among them, they like me some- times, and laugh at me sometimes, yet never know what I am doing.[25]

And he might well have added that they never will know. For, poet though he was, Synge naïvely assumed, as do we all, that his mere symbolic knowing could somehow be reconciled, also symbolically, with the rhythm and the music that indicate the primary integrative function of all living processes. No, they could not "know," for, after all, the poet *was* a waif, a wanderer in a "normal" world of images and symbols that had lost their savor. Like the rest of mankind who have become civilized and accustomed to symbolic or image knowing, Synge searched everywhere for a mood that is consonant, found it momentarily in this sea-girt people "in the intonation of a few sentences or some old fragment of melody," only to reject it in favor of his accustomed symbolic knowing, his will.

It is no wonder, then, that he should say: "there is hardly an hour I am with them that I do not feel the shock of some inconceivable idea. . . ." Not only was it a shock, but, as in his dream, an "uncontrollable frenzy" that leaves his battered organism trembling in the midst of this "perfect home" and the moonlight on the sea. The preconscious, the preacquisitive, larval mode of living organisms is of its nature exclusive of the projective idea, the "you" and "I," the "right" and "wrong," or the otherness implied in *looking at* on the basis of man's image-intercourse. But, like all other human beings, Synge goes on searching, searching for a symbol, an *idea* of unity, searching everywhere with never-ceasing clash and shock—everywhere except within the primary integrative processes of his own physiological organism, the primary physiological organism of man as a race.

Phylobiological observations over many years warrant the view that, throughout the species, there is nothing more common in man's present behavior than his propensity to replace with mere outer, detached, rationalized images of unity those integrated physiological reactions that constitute the emergence in adult life of his early larval identification with the maternal organism. Throughout society, there is a marked absence of a generically organized basis of thinking and feeling that is physiologically integrative. Accordingly, the single individual has recourse only to a secondary, symbolic mechanism —a mechanism that characterizes the adaptive behavior of society generally—and thus he *projects* the image of a personal "home" or "nest." In other words, seeking this purely esoteric escape, he automatically regresses, or falsely integrates, toward a symbolic representation of his original prenatal basis of unity.

Needless to say, in the organism's progression from its original unitary, confluent mode to its present adult, "normal" status in a complex society of organisms, much has happened to deflect the biophysical course of the individual's primal, integrative processes. If we may judge from our present widespread engrossment in symbolic standards of adaptation and their arbitrary emphasis on conflict as a primary motivation, it would seem impossible to recognize, much less regain, man's original biophysical prerogative—his total mode of bionomic adaptation as a phylum. But, from the scattered examples presented here, the student may sense, at least in part, how this primary total organization of living processes, with their basis in an early confluent, larval mode, is reflected socially in a certain organic sensitization or "awareness" redolent of the primary mode.

Though it is obvious that, in its original physiological state, this preconscious mode quite excludes all symbolic or ideational content—all social or interindividual exchange as we now know and utilize it in adult years—the premental sphere of expression or of feeling is not without its avenues of communication. If it has inadvertently happened that only what is ideational is now preponderantly operative interindividually in the species man, this does not necessarily mean that the preideational life of man, with its primary needs and feelings, has not also its communicable forms of expression among the elements that comprise human society. It does mean, however, that man's sensitivity to his own original preconscious mode of awareness can be recognized now only through the smoke and clouds of his present symbolic form of exchange—and then only as a symptom.

NOTES

1. *Psychology of Early Childhood up to the Sixth Year of Age* (New York: Henry Holt and Company, 1924), p. 505.

2. "Environmental Forces," in Carl Murchison, ed., *A Handbook of Child Psychology* (2nd ed., Worcester, Mass.: Clark University Press, 1933), p. 619.

3. *The Story of an African Farm* (Boston: Little Brown and Company, 1915), p. 154.

4. *Social Behavior and Child Personality* (New York: Columbia University Press, 1937), p. 290.

5. "Gentle" is derived from the Old French, *gentil,* "belonging to the same clan." It is allied to "genus."

6. *Op. cit.,* pp. 269 f.

7. "Human Infancy and the Ontogenesis of Behavior," *American Scientist,* 37 (1949), 529–553.

8. "Le Sens de la propriété chez les enfants," *Journal de Psychologie Normale et Pathologique,* 35 (1938), 245–262.

9. "L'Évolution psychique de l'enfant," in R. Debré, *Cours de Pediatrie Sociale* (Paris: Médicales Flammarion, 1949), pp. 799–812.

   Cp. Norman Kelman, "Character Development in Young Children," *American Journal of Psychoanalysis,* 10 (1950), 5–17.

10. Rafael Karsten, "Blood Revenge, War, and Victory Feasts among the Jibaro Indians of Eastern Ecuador," *U.S. Bureau of American Ethnology, Bulletin* 79 (1923), pp. 11 f.

11. Th. W. Danzel, *Kultur und Religion des primitiven Menschen* (Stuttgart: Strecker und Schroeder, 1924), p. 52.

12. Elsden Best, *The Maori* (Wellington, N.Z.: The Board of Maori Ethnological Research, 1924), I, 397 f.

13. William C. Willoughby, *Race Problems in the New Africa* (Oxford: Clarendon Press, 1923).

14. Alfred Storch, *The Primitive Archaic Forms of Inner Experiences and Thought in Schizophrenia* (New York and Washington: Nervous and Mental Disease Monograph Series No. 36, 1924), pp. 32 f.

15. Lucien Lévy-Bruhl, *The "Soul" of the Primitive* (New York: Macmillan Co., 1928).

16. *The Great Transformation* (New York: Farrar & Rinehart, 1944), p. 46.

17. (Boston: The Page Company, 1892), pp. 293 f.
    Cp. Robert Redfield, *The Primitive World and its Transformations* (Ithaca: Cornell University Press, 1953).

18. *Instinct and the Unconscious* (Cambridge: Cambridge University Press, 1920), p. 95.

19. *Op. cit.*, pp. 297 f.

20. Louis Roule, *Fishes*, "Their Journeys and Migration," trans. Conrad Elphinstone (London: George Routledge & Sons, 1933), pp. 34–103, 196–242; J. R. Norman, *A History of Fishes* (New York: Frederick A. Stokes Company, 1931), pp. 285–291.

21. *Op. cit.*, pp. 31, 74.

22. Cp. Burrow, "The Heroic Rôle—An Historical Retrospect," *Psyche*, VI (1926), 42–54.

23. *The Aran Islands* (Boston: John W. Luce and Co., 1911), pp. 103 f.; reprinted by permission of Bruce Humphries, Boston.

24. *Ibid.*, p. x.

25. *Ibid.*, pp. 120 f.

9

Toward Man's
Maturity

The reader will have gathered that the tendency of the pre-conscious mode is not what one would ordinarily call "up and doing." Nevertheless, he will doubtless have also observed that this primal mode or phase is historically by no means negligible when we come to reckon with the genetic data of human consciousness. From the standpoint of evolution, the organic confluence of the primordial principle of identification with the experiences of maturity constitutes a most important determinant in the mental and emotional life of individual and phylum. The recognition of the primary mode of consciousness opens an indispensable avenue of correlation between the processes of the individual's conscious development and the incidental disharmonies of his mental life. Likewise, this recognition provides a means of correlating the primary life of the species as a whole with man's present social symbols and world-wide disaffections.

We have under consideration a mechanism whereby the organism of man, unlike that of other animals, passes from a primary phase of total physiological subjectivity and continuity to a phase of mentally objective or symbolic "awareness," first in respect to others and then to itself. In this mechanism, there occur the first stages of a process of adjustment, of an organic emergence, that is primarily integrative and physiological.

But, unlike other animals in their adaptive progress, man's organism is thrust forward into a new and relatively untried field of adaptation. Total, integrative processes are newly summoned to a venture that will put to a test the primary authority of the organism's basic totality. For in the process of coming to "see" with greater *objective* definition, the infant organism comes also, through almost imperceptible changes, to see its outer world as though in its "seeing" it were necessarily looking across a barrier. The element of otherness is introduced. Within an originally subjective, unified premise of action, an organic cleavage takes place. A secondary, symbolic function is developed within the infant's totally organized structure, and there is launched a biological trend consisting of total process plus secondary process, which, according as integration prevails or is retarded, determines the organism's later health or dysfunction.

In a very true sense, all life, all nature, consists in conformity to a fitting or correct principle of conduct. We see its operation in animals. It is the law of growth on every hand. Everywhere there is the healthy, constructive, *right* process, as over against the process that is destructive, disordered, or *wrong*. The healthy human infant represents the acme of what is right. It sleeps seasonably; its food intake and elimination are properly regulated. The infant's muscular coordination, its space sense, and the gradually increasing excursions of its interest and activities—all this is right, all this is fitting, all this is biologically sound and healthy.

In the specialization of the external senses associated with the process of symbolic mentation, we see again a development that is biologically sound and fitting. But there seems to have occurred also the concomitant projection of the organism of others as though these organisms were organically alien to and discontinuous with oneself. There results a complex of organically divisive phenomena whose external counterpart is reflected symptomatically in conflicting social images and relationships.[1] This divisive trend inculcated afresh in each generation affects man's own internal processes.

As I sense this intrinsic condition—a condition to which my attention has been led through the analysis, not only of individuals, but also of groups—there has occurred a physiological breach in the natural continuity existing throughout the species. This breach—which man now only *senses*, and as yet but vaguely, as an ineptness of function internal to himself—is organically intolerable to the organism, whether phylum or individual. It is innately characteristic of man that he struggles constantly to recover his primary organic basis and restore his physiological integrity of function as a phylum by reuniting the individuals or elements that constitute its integral structure. But the separate, individuated element, having already grown unconsciously habituated to its newly acquired mental or projective system of images and relationships, persists in adhering to its merely symbolic, projective paths of inter-individual contact and affinity.

Thus, through its own individuated autogeny of function, man's organism becomes isolated and confined within the limitations of its symbolic, projected processes. Inevitably, therefore, he now employs the projective senses or the image only to defeat the efforts of the organism as a whole to re-center and reintegrate its total basis of reaction as a phylum.

Accordingly, the separate individual fashions a mental image of harmony and unity which he automatically projects outside himself toward the person or organism presumably existing apart from and opposite himself. But this wishful fantasy of unity vainly attempts to render the organism substitute service for the basic, intrinsic harmony of function of which it has been deprived. This fanciful unity is represented in man's philosophies, religions, and systems of morality which give the name of "right" to the purely symbolic effort of the organism to re-establish its harmonious communication and contact.

We are first brought to a symbolic sense of what is right—to a "knowing" appreciation of the difference between "right" and "wrong"—in early childhood. The studies of social reactions in our experimental group settings give evidence that this sense of right which is invoked by the parent—by all parents —is not biological in the sense of conforming to the principle of action inherent in the healthy organism. In obedience to his or her own childhood training, the parent too frequently inculcates in the offspring a course of behavior that is based on private wish or advantage, on wishful social precepts in which personal convenience or advantage supersedes principles of community coordination and health. This mood of private personal rightness constitutes a serious flaw in the behavior of social man. In our present social interchange, "right" is not the biological prerogative we customarily think it is. It is a symbol that has lost contact with the actuality symbolized and that has come by accident to supplant the original authority or rightness constitutive of physiological wholeness—a wholeness which, to speak in terms of the phylum, is demonstrated "embryologically" in the total organic relation between the infant and the mother organism.

Inevitably, the overaccentuation of the symbol or the outer appearance of rightness has its counterpart in the merely peripheral, symbolic representations of unity, harmony, or wholeness that we see in the community. Consider, for instance, man's effort to achieve "peace." Despite an underlying physiological urge toward unification, peace with man, whether familial or international, represents an adjustment that is limited to those symbolic reactions that constitute his external behavior. There is an effort to "settle differences," as we say, wherein the very words imply a "bargain" in social images and a magnifying of the very "difference" that takes place in the infant organism when for the first time it begins to "look at" the mother organism as if across a barrier.

Under these conditions, it is not surprising that there exists socially a hodgepodge of individual relationships—misunderstandings, contradictory feelings and impressions, love in the form of ownership, jealousies, petty competitions, proprietary affections, and equally proprietary aversions. It is not surprising that there are the constant incentives at one time to dictatorship, at another to servility, with all the irritation and disaffection which we not only see but which we ourselves, both as individuals and as nations, feel subjectively.

In the absence of a common biological sense of right in respect to his behavior, man can hardly escape the prediction of Leonardo da Vinci when he said: "The works of men's hands will become the cause of their death." Mankind is in the grip of a vast mood-contagion. We are like the distraught community described by Dostoevsky in the prophetic dream of Raskolnikov,

> He dreamt that the whole world was condemned to a terrible new strange plague that had come to Europe from the depths of Asia. . . . Some new sorts of microbes were attacking the bodies of men, but these microbes were endowed with intelligence and will. Men attacked by them at once became mad and furious. But never had men considered themselves so intellectual and so completely in possession of the truth as these sufferers, never had they considered their decisions, their scientific conclusions, their moral convictions so infallible. Whole villages, whole towns and peoples went mad from the infection. All were excited and did not understand one another. Each thought that he alone had the truth and was wretched looking at the others. . . . They did not know how to judge and could not agree what to consider evil and what good; they did not know whom to blame, whom to justify. . . . They gathered together in armies against one an-

other, but even on the march the armies would begin attacking one another, the ranks would be broken and the soldiers would fall on each other. The alarm bell was ringing all day long in the towns; men rushed together, but why they were summoned and who was summoning them no one knew. The most ordinary trades were abandoned, because everyone proposed his own ideas, his own improvements, and they could not agree. The land too was abandoned. Men met in groups, agreed on something, swore to keep together, but at once began on something quite different from what they had proposed. They accused one another, fought and killed each other. There were conflagrations and famine. All men and all things were involved in destruction. The plague spread and moved further and further. Only a few men could be saved in the whole world.[2]

Today, in his separate mood of arbitrary rightness, man is mad. As he goes on with his image patchwork and clings tenaciously to the detached and divisive symbol, there is approximated ever more closely a state of world-wide behavioral conflict and neurosis such as that envisaged in the prescient dream of Dostoevsky's hero. In face of this world neurosis, science is confronted with its supreme challenge. If man is to reason sanely, he must take scientific reckoning of his own disordered processes. In the issues of today, debate has reached an impasse. Like the people in Raskolnikov's dream, we shall turn on and destroy one another unless science steps in and single-mindedly focuses on an objective consideration of this conflict of *my* right versus *your* right—a conflict that is at this very moment confounding the intelligent processes of mankind. When there are confederations of scientists earnestly studying *within themselves* this divisive mood currently motivating the behavior of social communities, there will automatically develop a confederacy of nations devoted no less earnestly to the common cause of a common inquiry *within themselves*. The time has come for decisive, disinterested analysis of *ourselves* as a race or species.[3]

In the test tube of human behavior represented by our

experimental group, the analysis of this symbolic, wishful sense of right—man's habitual but inconsistent behavioral criterion —became the very crux of our approach to the problem of human relations. Setting aside all questions as to whether this one or that one was "right," we turned to the phenomenon of rightness, of the projected affect and the private, wishful advantage inseparable from it, as exemplifying a state of mind affecting both sides equally. On this basis, we sought to analyze, to define, the *substance* of this mood or sensation that each of us experiences subjectively as *his* "right."

As we progressed with our study, we found that the sense or sensation of right is part and parcel of a systematized core of affects and prejudices present in each individual and determining his symbolic or projective social interaction. It was demonstrated that this systematized core of affects and prejudices incites in each individual a competitive drive in the interest of the self that is as socially divisive as it is persistent. I have called this core of affects and prejudices man's false self, or "I"-persona. For a long time, the "I"-persona and its autocratic mood proved itself a match for all our efforts to reach and modify it. Our various attempts, valiant though they were, failed to dissipate this deep-seated social complex with its implicit "I"-versus-"you" dichotomy.

But we stuck to our consistent and unremitting study here and now of the customary affect projections existing among us as a group. The procedure involved the constant arrest of one's habitual tendency to project onto others the occasion for one's disordered feeling or affect. Irritation, for example, may occur at any moment and always seems to result from some happening *outside* the organism. One automatically attempts to relieve the irritation by blaming "the other fellow," by attempting to change his behavior. To do this is to be subjectively involved in symbolic "rightness," in affect. If affect is to be dealt with objectively, the first task is to block its projection. We must allay the reflex urge to look to the behavior of others in order to explain our hostile, aggressive, or sentimental moods. We must feel the intransigent mood as a condition internal to the organism.

Needless to say, such a complete challenge to our affective life resulted in a severe and common feeling of frustration among us. But, however uncomfortable at the time, this common sense of frustration led to significant relational responses that brought about within us a feeling-sense of the artificial systematization of affects and prejudices that makes up the individual's habitual personality-formation—the encapsulated "I"-persona.

Finally, we sensed the discrepancy in this pattern of adaptation to the point of experiencing the physiological stress and discomfort underlying it. This sensation of stress or tension was predominantly localized behind the eyes and in the fore-part of the head. Because this area plays such an important role in mediating affect and symbol, I have called it the affecto-symbolic segment. The internal recording of this stress proved to be a vital step in our phylobiological researches.

With this development, our work began to engage tangible, physiological processes. Mental and social conflict became increasingly reduced to a problem in internal tension and stress. For it developed that the cultivation of this internal perception of stress dissipated the customary preoccupation with self-reflective, affect-laden images of one's self and of others. Coincidently, there was brought about a reconstellation of tensional patterns. That is, when the attention was withdrawn from projectively focusing on external items of behavior and was directed instead to the uncomfortable stress and tension in the region of the head and eyes, there slowly came about the spontaneous reinstatement of a pattern of tension that was not predominantly localized, but was more evenly distributed throughout the organism.

There was thus established a differentiation between two contrasting patterns of internal tensional adjustment—patterns which proved to be consistently related to contrasting modes of external behavior. Where the tensions were concentrated about the eyes and the forepart of the head, the accompanying behavior was affective and prejudiced, and one's wishful, symbolic sense of "right and wrong" held full sway. This mode of adjustment, with its accompanying pattern of physiological tensions, I have called "ditention." Where the tensions were generally distributed throughout the body and there was relaxation in the affecto-symbolic segment, the behavior was direct and objective. One's inveterate sense of "rightness" and the prejudice that accompanies it were absent. I have called this mode "cotention," since it resulted in consensual and coordinated social relations.

In inducing cotention, one does not *do* something; one undoes something—the pattern of the "I"-persona. This discarding is not for the purpose of bringing about a life of selflessness. That is mere sentimentality. Quite the contrary, cotention is the expansion of the sense of self to its phylic proportions. It is the achievement of an intelligent, comprehensive sense of the self that is biologically continuous with the social and physical environment. In recovering this basic pattern of behavior, one is merely carrying the law of evolution into the subjective domain of human feeling and motivation, now distorted by the untruth and superstition of ditention and neurosis.

Early in the physiological phase of our experimentation, we noted a marked difference in the rates of respiration accompanying the two attentional patterns. This observation led to an extensive series of instrumental measurements of physiological functions in those investigators who had had sufficient training to shift from one pattern to the other in a given experimental session. In addition to respiratory differences, there were found to be substantial and consistent differences in number and extent of eye movements and in brain-wave patterns in the ditentive as against the cotentive type of adaptation.* In cotention, the breathing is slower and deeper, the eyes are steadier, and there is a marked change in brain-wave pattern in the parietal or motor area. This change consists in a reduction in the amplitude of the alpha waves and in the percentage time of the alpha rhythm. Control experiments indicate that these changes are specific to cotention and that they occur automatically as an integral part of the cotentive response. The objective records of these altered patterns of functioning that distinguish cotention are of significance in that they give a physiological background to the striking modification in mood and motivation characterizing this behavioral mode.

I realize that my thesis is not easy to grasp mentally. In our accustomed symbolic outlook, we all have our convictions. We "know" all there is to know about human behavior purely from the background of the part-expression of the organism represented by the intellect and the symbol. But, unlike the writer and reader in their customary relationship, we are here not conferring *about* a problem observable outside ourselves. Quite the contrary. As living, quickened, neurodynamic organisms, my reader and I are one in our structure and function with the species we are here attempting to bring to objective study.

In our group work, we have attempted to negate the undue emphasis placed on purely intellectual factors and mental convictions. We have attempted to place our primary emphasis on the whole organism and on *feeling*, or the primary expression of the total organism. We have found that man's feeling— the feeling of every you and every me—is seriously disturbed and unbalanced. We have found that it has become unduly restricted in function and displaced from its primary seat within the organism-as-a-whole. Through our group approach,

* The complete results of the instrumental studies to date, including numerous charts and graphs, are contained in an appendix to *Science and Man's Behavior, op. cit.*, pp. 487–523.—Ed.

we have attempted to get an internal and generic appreciation of this disorder in our feeling life and to see how it determines our behavior, our thinking, our perception, and our convictions.

On the basis of results obtained in our intensive study of group behavior, the fundamental factor responsible for our individual and social conflicts is not to be found in the sphere of the idea and the symbol, nor can it be reached through them. The common factor underlying the varied symptomatology of behavior appears to be an imbalance in physiological functioning occasioned by the attempt to mediate whole processes of feeling through the restricted, projective avenues of image and symbol. This circumstance entails a serious inadequacy in the process of attention as it mediates man's relation to man. Instead of being related to his fellows cotentively, on the basis of common feeling, he is now related to them ditentively, on the basis of a system of separate affects and prejudices. Ditention is a disorder of function that destroys man's sense of his unity and solidarity as a species and sets each individual or each ideologically amalgamated group or nation against every other individual or nation as a separate and discrete entity. The private assumption of each of us that he possesses a valid "right" or prerogative and that other people are "right" only in the measure in which they agree with him is concomitant to this ditentive mechanism.

Our researches indicate the need of man to get an internal, physiological appreciation of his disorder—to *feel* the localized stress that is the inseparable somatic accompaniment of his emotional projections or affects. We know very well the physiological tensions that accompany individual states of ill health. We know, for example, the physiological stress or tension of an individual's revulsion as expressed in the reaction of nausea. But we do not appreciate the contrast in physiological tensions that accompany man's healthy and his unhealthy social relations. We do not feel the internal difference between one's falsely separate sense of identity (the "I"-

persona) and the sense of our common identity as an organismic race or species. I do not think we shall heal the pain of our individual and international differences except as we learn to define within ourselves the presence of these contrasting patterns and thus learn to discriminate the divisive from the integrative behavioral mode.

Common laws and principles are operative throughout nature. Through these laws and principles, phenomena are related effectively and meaningfully. Whether in physics, astronomy, or ecology, there is a coordination of the interacting parts into a totality of structure and function. By and large, electrons and protons react in an orderly way; the stars remain within their appointed orbits; and an effective balance is maintained among the various species of organism and their environments. It is only in the field of human behavior that this primary orderliness does not seem to apply. It is only in man's relation to man that there exists confusion worse confounded. It is only here that we see impasse and over-all destructive trends. But, as C. Judson Herrick once wrote me:

> The world is not mad. It is only the people in it who are mad. The world is orderly, and even human madness is lawfully ordered. It has causes and consequences which can be discovered and ameliorated.

It is the growing view of men of science that there can be no question as to the inherent unity of human groups throughout the world. In *Mirror for Man,* the anthropologist Clyde Kluckhohn remarks: "The members of all human groups have about the same biological equipment."[4] And the renowned physiologist A. J. Carlson has said:

> We hear much today about "One World," but not enough about "One Human Species." At least we do not always act, at home or abroad, as if we believed this proved biologic fact.[5]

The problem of human behavior is universal. Whatever our profession, whatever our nationality, creed, or philosophy, it is time that we forego our aloofness and recognize our part in a problem that is equal and common to man. Relinquishing the role of specialists, we need to take hold of a problem that involves the biophysical adjustment of the organism of man to its environment, an environment that is social as well as biological. Our phylobiological studies indicate that, when man consistently circumvents his habitual symbolic interrelationships—his customary affect projections—through a physiological technique in tensional readjustment, he automatically reverts to behavior that is common and unified. Regaining alignment with preconscious foundations, he becomes motivated in relation to an organismic compactness and solidarity that inheres both in the organism of the individual and in the species of which that individual is an inseparable element.

This principle of commonness and solidarity underlying mature consciousness and motivation is a scientific finding that man needs to reaffirm in his own internal processes. Only thus will we attain the altered frame of reference requisite to a science of man's behavior and stem the tide of the most widespread and communicable of all diseases.

NOTES

1. Trigant Burrow, "Social Images versus Reality," *The Journal of Abnormal Psychology and Social Psychology*, XIX (1924), 230–235.
2. *Crime and Punishment*, trans. Constance Garnett (New York: The Macmillan Co., 1917), pp. 489 f.; reprinted with permission of The Macmillan Co. and William Heinemann, Ltd., London.
3. A five-year plan entailing a world truce in which man would be afforded the opportunity for an examination of conscience (origi-

nally meaning "consciousness") would, I believe, not be without productive value to a world whose processes, personal and social, have reached an impasse in which no solution offers itself outside these same disordered processes.

4. (New York: Whittlesey House, 1949), p. 20.

5. "Science, Education, and the Future of Man," *Scientific Monthly,* 65 (1947), 502.

ACKNOWLEDGMENTS

Chapter 3 was a paper read at the fifth annual meeting of the American Psychoanalytic Association, New York City, May 4, 1915, and published in *The Psychoanalytic Review*, V (1918), 243–254. Reprinted through the courtesy of the editors and the publisher, National Psychological Association for Psychoanalysis, Inc.

Chapter 4 is composed of a chapter written in 1918 for the first draft of *The Preconscious* and sections of an unpublished paper, "Psychoanalysis and Life," read in 1913 before the New York Academy of Medicine.

Chapter 5 was read in abstract at the seventh annual meeting of the American Psychoanalytic Association, Boston, May 25, 1917.

Chapter 9 contains some material from an unpublished paper written about 1948.

INDEX